Dedication

To my husband Hugh

and

to my family

for

their encouragement and support.

Rocks in Her Head or How I Became a Rolling Stone

HELEN LISS IVANHOE SMART

Helen Liss Ivanhoe Smart
1106-B Calle de los Amigos
Santa Barbara, CA 93105
805-770-2033
hughsmart@aol.com

 www.trafford.com

North America & international
toll-free: 1 888 232 4444 (USA & Canada)
fax: 812 355 4082

CONTENTS

The Upheaval

When Ann Landers was asked, "What makes a successful marriage?" she replied, "When the rocks in her head fit the holes in his."

An apt description for the wife of a geologist, but it took me forty-five years to realize that neither my rocks nor his holes could be ground to fit.

In the beginning, in 1949, we were a stable family, a father with a secure job as a geologist with Standard Oil of California, a mother who was a part-time teacher in the Kern County school system, and two young children, a three-year-old girl and a five-year-old boy. Cheryl and Rod were my husband's children from a previous marriage, and Buster, my husband, adored them both.

"My Cheryl is beautiful. The boys will swarm around her like bees to honey."

But it was his son, Rod, on whom he lavished his praises and hopes.

"This boy is brilliant. He will be famous. He is talented, sharp, perceptive, and clever. He's smarter than any child I've ever known. Rod is a genius. I feel sorry for parents who do not have children as exceptional as Rod and Cheryl."

Our family life began in Taft, a hot, dry, dusty, bleak, desert oil town in the Southern San Joaquin Valley of Central California. When Standard Oil transferred us to Bakersfield two years later, we were delighted to live where there were big shady trees, blooming shrubs, green lawns, and well-kept streets. Always eager to make more money, Buster decided we could accomplish our goal by buying run-down properties, upgrading them, then offering them for rent. So landlords we became. Because my husband was often out of town on business, the upkeep and managing of our rentals became my responsibility.

It was a Friday afternoon. I was atop a high ladder, stapling acoustical tile across the discolored, peeling ceiling of our latest acquisition, feeling very triumphant because I had managed to nail the furring strips to which the tiles would be stapled twelve inches apart across the whole ceiling all by myself. The two rows of acoustical tiles that I had stapled so far looked fresh and clean. Eager to keep working, I stopped when I saw a tall stranger bounding into the room.

"Mrs. Ivanhoe?" he called out.

"Yes."

"Your son is a thief," he unceremoniously blurted out.

The heavy stapler slipped from my hands and fell to the floor with a bang.

"Your son is in jail. I'm a private detective hired by the Bakersfield High School, and I've been trying to nail this kid for six months. He's been stealing chemicals from the high school lab all that time. What kind of a mother are you? Don't you know what your kid is doing?"

That evening I had the difficult task of phoning my absent husband with the shocking news.

"I'm to go to juvenile hall tomorrow to talk to the authorities. I'll call you when I know more."

Once before, I had been to juvenile hall, but that time as a substitute teacher. Never, never, never could I have imagined I would visit as the heartsick mother of an inmate. When I arrived at the hall, everyone was very gracious to me. I was ushered into a room where a kindly-looking man sat behind a huge desk. He stood up when I entered.

"Please sit down, Mrs. Ivanhoe. We have sent for your son. He'll be here shortly."

I had been determined not to cry, but when they brought Rod in dressed in prison garb, an olive drab jumpsuit, ill-fitting and much too big, hanging loosely on his small frame, he looked so little and helpless. His head hung down and his eyes were red. I began to cry.

"I'm sorry. I didn't mean to cry."

"Most mothers do," the man replied gently as he reached in a drawer and handed me a box of Kleenex.

Shock. Tears. Anger. Sorrow. Recriminations. Bewilderment from two saddened parents. Rod and a friend of his admitted to stealing chemicals from the high school lab. Their goal?

"We wanted to make an atom bomb."

Rod was put on six months probation and required to report to his probation officer every three weeks.

Buster was a devastated father.

"I am so ashamed. I can no longer face my family and my friends. This has been on the radio, in the newspapers here and even in Canada. I cannot live in Bakersfield any longer. We are going to move!"

And move we did. In 1961 we became gypsies moving from place to place with no permanent home. We were Cygani (gypsies) for the next twenty years.

Getting Ready to Roll

We had lived ten years in Bakersfield, long enough to put down roots, long enough to have a wide circle of interesting friends, long enough to be actively involved in community affairs, long enough to have a feeling of belonging.

That all ended. The day we sold our house, I feared that our lives would never be stable again. We became gypsies, moving from rental to rental in Southern California.

Disgusted and discouraged with everything and everyone, my husband quit his oil company job as a geologist and decided to be on his own as an independent oil consultant geologist-geophysicist.

"Now I'm free to go anywhere I'm called." But no one called him, and Buster became increasingly irritable, morose, and bitter, often angrily denouncing his son.

"How could Rod do this to me?"

The son he had idolized and glorified had shattered his father's dreams. If I tried to talk to Buster about Rod, he withdrew.

"You can't possibly understand my pain. You are a stepmother. I'm his father. I'm the one suffering."

Determined to find work somewhere, anywhere, Buster pursued his dream of becoming an international petroleum consultant. Day after day, he sent out his lengthy résumés to oil companies across America. He expanded his job search to Europe and Asia. He made phone calls to any geologist or geophysicist he had ever heard of. Each day he waited eagerly for the mailman and rushed to answer a ringing telephone. No luck for weeks. Then it finally happened!

When a phone call came from Tel Aviv, inquiring whether Buster was available to immediately come to Israel, the answer was a resounding, "Yes!"

In the following years, Buster made numerous regular trips from California to Israel. His work was challenging; he admired the progress made by the Israelis, and they appreciated the honesty of his reports.

This job had opened the door to others, and soon, Buster was involved in oil exploration worldwide, culminating in an extensive trip from Israel to the Middle East and on to the Orient. His self-respect had returned, and he was a pleasanter man.

In 1963, after various moves across Southern California, we had established ourselves in an apartment in Beverly Hills. It was late on a November morning when Laura, my next-door neighbor, knocked on my front door. I opened it to see a weeping woman.

"What is wrong? What is it?"

"President Kennedy has been shot," she sobbed.

It was a moment I would never forget.

Cheryl had graduated from Beverly Hills High School and enrolled at California Lutheran College in Thousand Oaks. Rod's grandparents in Iowa had asked for Rod to come and live with them. I was alone so much that my neighbors began to wonder if I was widowed or divorced or if I had ever married.

"This husband you speak of, is he real or a figment of your imagination?"

To occupy my time, I had enrolled in adult education classes at the Beverly Hills High School. In early December, one of the men in class stood up and made an announcement.

"I'm suing the City of Los Angeles. They leave the City Hall lights on all night in the form of a cross. That's using public funds to promote a religion, so I'm suing."

"But this is a Christian country," I blurted out.

The lady sitting in front of me turned and looked at me.

"How long have you lived here, honey?"

Until then I had not realized that Beverly Hills was predominantly a Jewish community.

A welcome letter arrived from Buster in the spring of 1964.

"Helen, I have just signed a long-term contract with Lapidoth Oil Company, headquartered in Tel Aviv. Why don't you close up our apartment and join me? The pay won't be much; we'll have to cover our own lodging and meals, but it will be a chance for you to see this remarkable country. You'll have to sell your little yellow Mustang and check with our attorney friend in Bakersfield to determine what else you must do."

My mind raced. Fill out change of address cards for the fourth time in three years. Pack. Sort. Call the movers. Sell the car. A friend bought my Mustang as a high school graduation present for his son. Later I learned that the son had totaled the car in an accident within three months.

My beautiful little yellow Mustang was now a heap of "junk."

Our attorney friend in Bakersfield met with me. "You seem to have covered all bases for your extended trip to Israel, but there is one important thing you must do."

"What is that?"

"How old is Cheryl?" he asked.

"She is eighteen."

"Helen, the age of majority in California is still twenty-one, so in your absence, you must have a court-appointed person with power of attorney to make any legal decisions for Cheryl. What if she needs medical care? Or a blood transfusion? Helen, this is something you must do before you leave the country."

As I stood up to leave, our attorney's parting words were very sobering.

"Pick someone you trust because that person will have more authority over Cheryl than you have ever had. Buster has never allowed you to legally adopt his children."

A test of true friendship and loyalty is the person who will voluntarily agree to have power of attorney over a friend's eighteen-year-old. Doris and Jim were such friends.

When I told Doris how grateful I was to her and to Jim, I said, "I couldn't be going to Israel without you."

"Then how come you are?" Doris laughed.

The weight limit on overseas checked baggage was a very strict forty-five pounds. I had devoted much time to figuring out how I could carry on extra items. My coat pockets were stuffed with heavier things, my huge purse was crammed, two garment bags were draped, one over each arm, the left one hiding a heavy shoulder bag.

"You look like a walking pile of things." Doris smiled when she and Jim saw me off at the Los Angeles International Airport.

Finally, I was on my way to Israel.

CHAPTER

3

Israel, the First Bounce

Europe was familiar to me. In 1957, I had been on a three-month study tour of the continent. Flying in those days was very expensive. The only affordable choice across the Atlantic was by ship, a five-day voyage. Now here I was crossing the same ocean in a matter of hours, off to a land I'd heard of since childhood. Every seat on that El Al airplane was occupied by enthusiastic passengers who never stopped talking, eagerly voicing their anticipation of soon being in the land of their forefathers. Their excitement was obvious, as was mine.

When the captain announced, "We'll be landing at Lod Airport soon. Please stay in your seats until the plane has come to a complete stop and I have turned off the seat belt sign," several passengers jumped up and began reaching into the overhead bins.

"Stay in your seats!" the stewardess ordered sharply. "Stay in your seats until the captain has turned off the seat belt sign."

My seatmate, a middle-aged lady from New York City took a deep breath.

"Oh! I can already feel the freedom in the air," she happily exclaimed.

The very instant the plane touched the ground, the clicking sound of seat belts being unfastened filled the plane as all the passengers jumped up to reclaim their overhead luggage.

"Sit down! Sit down!" the stewardess kept loudly repeating. "Remain seated until the plane has come to a complete stop and the captain has turned off the seat belt sign. Sit down! Sit down! Sit down!"

No one listened. The stewardess gave up.

The airport bus into the city passed by a cluster of big trees on the left side of the road. Underneath those trees a large number of scruffy people appeared to be living under the canopy. Clothing hung from the branches, cooking equipment was stacked on the ground, makeshift chairs were scattered about. Several grubby little children clung to their mother's skirts. The whole area had the look of a cluttered permanent encampment.

When I embarked from the bus, I asked the driver, "Who are those people living in that encampment we passed?"

"What encampment? I didn't see any encampment," he replied. My first lesson in Israeli politics.

Our hotel was a modest building facing a peaceful blue Mediterranean. Our upstairs balcony gave us a view of the big luxury hotel next door and a sweeping view of the wide clean beaches on either side. Behind us the city of Tel Aviv. I looked forward to exploring the town. Each morning, after my husband eagerly left for work, I was on my own to do as I pleased.

For the next several days, I wandered about trying to decipher the strange letters on the street signs, stopping to taste the unfamiliar new foods sold by the street vendors—falafel, humus, tahina, couscous, pita bread, and roasted chickpeas. No one bothered me or paid any attention to me.

Restaurants were limited in the city in 1964, but each evening my husband and I managed to find a place to eat, often eating at a place on Ditzengoff Circle that displayed a plate with the evening's special in the window. One evening it was a plate with two almond-shaped pieces of meat, labeled in big print.

"Eggs of the male cow."

"What is that?" I asked my husband.

"It's bull's testicles. You are an adventuresome eater. Why don't you try it?"

When the plate arrived, there were two small almond-shaped pieces of meat, no salad, no vegetables, no rice or bread, just those two unappetizing-looking blobs on a big white plate. I stared at the offering and pushed it aside.

"Aren't you going to eat it?" my husband asked.

"I can't. I would feel like a cannibal."

Each day I boarded a local bus to explore place-names I had heard of since I was a child. Busy, bustling Jerusalem, everywhere ancient gates and monuments, narrow crowded streets, laden donkeys, bearded men and robed women—the whole city was a fascinating museum and there was never enough time before I had to stop to catch the bus back to Tel Aviv. The Wailing Wall intrigued me as I watched the bobbing heads of the praying men. Where were the women?

Listening to the informative and interesting Jerusalem tour guides was always a learning experience.

"Today," one young guide announced, "we are going to an area of the city we don't often visit. We're taking you to an ultraorthodox area of Jerusalem called Mia Sharim, a very religious neighborhood."

He smiled. "But I must forewarn you, we may not receive a cordial reception."

We didn't. Small boys tossed clods of dirt at our bus, shouting loudly as they ran alongside our slow-moving vehicle.

"It's nothing personal," our guide explained. "The residents of Mia Sharim do not like any outsiders traveling through their neighborhood, not tourists, not Israeli citizens, not visitors, not anyone."

In a sunny doorway, I watched a young man, dressed in a long black coat and a broad-brimmed black hat, sitting listlessly, twirling his thick, black, long side curls, occasionally stopping to scratch himself.

This group was in glaring contrast to the friendly industrious Israelis I had been meeting in Tel Aviv.

But nothing impressed me like the Garden of Gethsemane. As I stood in the ancient, quiet olive orchard, I thought, "Jesus may have stood here in this very spot two thousand years ago. Maybe Jesus leaned against this very same gnarled tree."

By bus I visited the Dead Sea, then climbed up Masada. From atop the rock, I looked down at the outline of the Roman encampments, where the Roman soldiers had waited to attack the last band of Jewish fighters about AD 72. History was all around me. Churches were everywhere dating back hundreds of years, and in every church, a request for money. In Bethlehem in front of the manger where Jesus is believed to have been born, a priest grabbed hold of my hand.

"Touch! Touch!" he whispered as he pushed my hand against the manger.

"Money! Money!" he grinned as he dropped my arm and held out his own palm.

Another bus ride took me to a British cemetery in the bleak, dry Negev Desert. When I opened the gate and stepped inside, I entered a green, immaculately manicured graveyard with tidy upright stones. Wandering among the graves, I read the names of the fallen, eighteen-, nineteen-, and twenty-year-olds from Australia and New Zealand, all buried so far from home when Britain fought Turkey. And for what? I was angered by the futility of war.

That anger returned another day when I was on a guided tour of the Negev. As we passed the British cemetery, the Israeli guide pointed out, "There is one Jewish boy buried in that cemetery."

"What about all the rest?" I thought.

In 1964, Israel was still a very young country. Every Israeli I met was proud of what had been accomplished since 1948, and their pride and dedication was deep and sincere. Some of them told us their memorable stories. I remember Kashi's story well.

Kashi was a young eighteen-year-old living in Poland before the start of World War II. The underground sent him a message.

"Get out immediately. The Gestapo are coming for you tonight. You have no time to lose."

Kashi glanced at his parents. They nodded their heads. He grabbed a knapsack and ran to his sixteen-year-old girlfriend's house.

"The Gestapo are coming tonight to get me. I'm going to try to get to Israel. Will you come with me?"

For a brief moment, she was silent.

"Yes!" was her positive reply.

Then she hurriedly hugged her parents, and the two of them dashed out the door into the night. She never saw her family again.

They made it to Israel. When we met them, we saw a loving, dedicated couple who were proud to be Israelis. Kashi and his wife often took my husband and me to small Arabic restaurants they favored where we ate "white meat." It was pork and tasted good, but we always referred to it as "white meat."

When we met Eli, he told us he had been released from a concentration camp when the Americans came.

"What was it like when you were finally freed?" I asked.

"Oh! I don't like to talk about it. I want to forget. If I talk about it, it all comes back."

After a brief silence, he continued, "I walked outside the fence, walked back into the prison, walked back out, back in, then finally realized I was free!"

In my wanderings, I talked with a young Palestinian lad who handed me a thin booklet called *The Resentful Arab*.

"Will you please read this?" he asked. "They took away my parent's home. If we want to go to Jerusalem to visit relatives, we have to get a travel permit."

I was left with an uneasy feeling that some things were not right, but I dared not say anything.

With time on my hands, I walked south to Jaffa and stopped at a slight rise where a deep pit was being dug. The young man at the bottom glanced up.

"What are you doing?" I called down.

"I'm an archaeologist, and I'm digging up ancient pottery shards. Want to help me?"

For the next week, I worked alongside this enthusiastic young man. He showed me how to find two shards that fit easily together, how to glue them, then stand them in sand to dry.

"I believe in Israel, but my wife won't come here. She's in New York City. I miss her, but I can't leave my homeland. My place is here."

Tour guards came by with their groups, pointing to us at the bottom of the pit.

"Here you see two dedicated Israeli archaeologists working to find evidence of our ancient history."

I smiled and remained silent.

After a week, I had found all the pieces of my little clay pot, glued them together, and triumphantly held up my finished clay bowl.

"Oh! Look! I have an ancient artifact to take back to America."

"I'm afraid not," my mentor replied. "This belongs to Israel and will go to one of our museums."

One evening, an American woman came to our hotel with an invitation.

"Would Helen like to join us? There are four of us ladies who drive out one day each week to the sand dunes of the ancient Roman ruins of Ashdod and Askelon and we look for Roman coins and glass shards."

I eagerly accepted. The winds that constantly blew across the dunes shifted the sands so that on our weekly treks, we always found some freshly exposed coins, mostly small and worn, but still real Roman coins. It was a thrill to reach down and pick up a coin almost two thousand years old. For an hour or so, we five ladies walked back and forth across the dunes, eyes peering down, enjoying the breeze and the solitude.

"That's Gaza over there," one of the ladies said, pointing to the west. "And over there in the other direction, we can see Jordan."

"How close these three countries are," I remarked.

From our hotel balcony, I could look down at the clean uncrowded beach below that looked like an inviting spot to lie quietly in the warm Israeli sun. Beach towel under my arm, I walked out to spend a relaxing few hours on the sand.

Lying peacefully listening to the gentle lapping of the clean blue Mediterranean waves, I had almost fallen asleep when a shadow brushed across my closed eyes.

"Hello," a male voice said.

"Oh, go away and leave me alone," I thought, but I did not stir or reply.

"Do you speak English?"

Again I gave no indication that I had heard or understood.

"Parlez vous Francais?"

Again I gave no answer.

"Habla usted Espanol?"

It was difficult not to laugh, but I remained stoic.

"Parla Italiano?"

No answer.

"Rozumieć Po Polsku?"

Still no answer.

Then an exasperated voice blurted out, "Don't you even speak Hebrew?"

That's when I could contain myself no longer. I sat up and laughed.

It was interesting to be an impartial observer on the beach to watch the people and overhear their comments.

Two ladies were chatting not far from me.

"Do you know how hard it is to eat Kosher in Tel Aviv?" one lady lamented.

Nearby two very handsome athletic young men were engaged in conversation.

"I've been here two months, and I've never had to pay for a meal. I meet ladies, make friends with them, and they take me to movies and plays and buy all my dinners just for being their companion—no strings attached."

"Don't you feel guilty?" his friend asked.

"Not at all," he replied. "These women are lonely. I fill a void."

Some people are subtle. Some people are direct. What could be more direct than the man who approached me one morning as I spread my beach towel on the sand.

"Good morning," he called out.

Then he unceremoniously knelt at the edge of my towel and, with no further preliminaries, spoke, "Oh, to hell with all this chit-chat. Let's just go to bed. No? Well, it was worth a try."

On the days that I had been on the beach, I had watched a very pretty, slender young lady wearing a very brief bikini.

Day after day, she paraded back and forth along the shore for several hours. My curiosity led me to ask, "Who is that lady?"

"Oh, that is Shlafka. She comes here every day hoping some rich American will see her and take her to New York."

Now forty-five years later, I wonder if Shlafka ever achieved her dream.

One morning in late September, I opened the blinds to see a dramatic change on the beach in front of our hotel. The waters of the Mediterranean that had been so blue and peaceful were now a seething mass of dark blue-black waves rising high as they noisily pounded the shore.

Summer was over. Our contract had ended. It was time to leave.

During the following years, my husband made many trips to Israel. He and an astute Israeli businessman Zvi Alexander worked closely together and became trusted friends and confidants. Zvi believed that because oil-producing countries surrounded Israel, there had to be oil somewhere within Israel. And L. F. Ivanhoe, geologist and geophysicist, believed he was the person to find it. Buzz, as he was called in Israel, and Zvi made secret trips to Athens, London, and Rome in an effort to raise funds for Israeli oil exploration. Oil exploration can be a cut-throat affair, competitive and ruthless, demanding absolute secrecy. In his book *Oil*, Zvi Alexander gives credit to Buzz for his dedicated efforts, even sharing a well-kept state secret with him. In 1966, only a few powerful people in Israel knew that Signal Oil Company of California owned one-third of an Israeli oil company at the same time it was producing oil in Kuwait. What? Israelis and Arabs doing business together?

Zvi was a humble man, comfortable to be with. The first time I met him, he told me a joke I have remembered for forty-five years.

"Helen, do you know the story of the man who jumped out of the Empire State Building? As he was passing the thirtieth floor, someone called out, 'How is it going?'

'So far so good,' the falling man replied."

It was almost twenty years later that I was able to spend some time in Israel. The changes within the country were startling. Our little hotel on the beach was gone. Now the whole Mediterranean shore was lined with luxury hotel after luxury hotel, each one grander and more beautifully landscaped than the last. The road from Tel Aviv to Jerusalem was now a superhighway. Red-roofed condos lined the road to Haifa. Everywhere I saw new houses and green lawns where barren soil had been twenty years ago.

When I had first seen the Wailing Wall, small houses occupied the crowded area in front of the busy wall. Now the houses were gone; a wide open space existed where people had once lived. Where had these people gone? And now it was called the Western Wall, a more gracious name.

One weekend during our visit, Zvi drove my husband and me around his country. His pride was obvious as he pointed out Israel's advances.

"We have come a long way these last twenty years. Look, Helen! We have fruit now. When you were here before, we had very little fruit, but look what we have now—lots of our own fruit."

He showed us a huge orchard, almost an acre, entirely encased in netting.

"We have to do this to keep out the bats. Before we put up the netting, they would come in every evening by the hundreds and devour our precious fruit. Before we leave, let's make sure this door is securely fastened because these clever creatures can find their way through the smallest opening."

Zvi drove us south across the Negev Desert. Where my American lady friends and I had walked the barren sand dunes of Ashdod and Askkelon, there were now two modern cities. I had seen Beersheba when it was a dirty main street with a dead rat in the middle of the road. Now it too was a modern town.

Off in the far, far distance, we could see the hazy outline of a gigantic domed building.

"What's that, Zvi?" Bus said with a mischievous grin.

"Gee, Buzz, I don't see anything," Zvi replied with a mischievous grin of his own.

Nothing more was said, but there seemed to be a silent understanding between the two men. Had they seen an atomic reactor? I wondered.

Over the years, we had kept in touch with Zvi and his wife, Rachel, visiting often and listening eagerly to Zvi's latest exploits around the world from Africa to Asia to America.

The last time we visited them in their posh London apartment, Zvi showed us a heavy necklace of rubies that he had purchased for Rachel in Burma.

"Oh! How gorgeous!" I exclaimed.

"But my wife won't wear them," Zvi lamented.

"They are so expensive, I'm afraid I will be robbed," Rachel replied.

CHAPTER
4

Moscow, the KGB, Polish Problems

"I suggest we not return to California at this time," my husband announced.

"There's an International Geological Conference in London that I want to attend, and the prospect of future work in this area looks good. Zvi Alexander wants me to return to Israel. Turkey may have work for me, and North Africa looks promising. Rome, Italy, is conveniently located as a headquarters for us. Why don't we visit there for a few weeks to see if we like it?"

With the help of Arthur Frommer's *Europe on 5 Dollars a Day*, we selected the centrally located Pensione Texas as our introduction to Rome.

On our first day in the Eternal City, we walked from the Termini, the central railroad station, to our hotel. We were immediately struck by the number of prostitutes of all ages lining the street in front of the Termini building.

One pretty young lady tugged at my husband's sleeve.

"American! American! Amore, Amore."

"Stop!" I blurted. "Go away. My husband."

"No problema. No problema." The unfazed young woman smiled.

Aggressive young gypsy girls dressed in long, colorful skirts, their faces sad and mournful, held out their hands as we walked by.

"Money! Money! Io, no mamma. No papa." (Me, no mother no father.)

In a burst of benevolence, I gave several coins to an especially convincing begging child; then suddenly, out of nowhere, a dozen small children emerged from the shadows, all of them with outstretched hands. A bold few began pulling at my skirt.

"Money! Money!" they called out in loud demanding voices.

"Let's get out of here," my husband shouted. "Welcome to Rome."

The Pensione Texas proved to be a good choice, clean, quiet, and pleasant.

Each morning we ate our crusty roll, drank our "caffe e latte" (coffee and milk) and headed off to explore a museum, often to be disappointed by "Chiuso para Riparazione" (Closed for Repairs). But there was always something new to be seen, an ancient monument, a Roman Forum, or an elaborate church that was in itself a museum. St. Peter's, that colossal building, dwarfed us by its immense size and awed us by its wealth of art. We could see weeks of sightseeing ahead of us.

When time came to leave for London to attend the geological gathering, we were almost reluctant to leave; so fascinated were we by Rome.

Conference over, we were wandering around London when we saw a travel poster, "Visit the USSR. See the Kremlin." Buster suggested, "We'll never be closer. Why don't we go?"

"Why not?" I replied. "We could go on to Poland and see where my parents came from." So several visas and copious amounts of paperwork and numerous delays later, we were off to the USSR. I wrote to my mother in Alberta with the address of a travel office in Warsaw where I hoped she would send us a letter with news of home.

When we landed at the airport of Moscow, our Aeroflot plane was the only plane on the tarmac. Not many tourists came to the USSR in 1965. A uniformed Intourist guide greeted us at the foot of the stairs as we embarked.

"Mr. and Mrs. Ivanhoe, I'm here to take you to your hotel."

The hotel was massive but bland. It's most memorable feature was the bathtub in our room: big, long, and deep but with no stopper. On the landing of our hotel floor, a dour-looking lady sat, each day suspiciously peering at us as we came and went. She acted as if we were unwanted intruders. But I felt a kinship with the people. They were Russian; I was Polish. We were both Slavs. They looked much like the immigrant neighbors near my father's homestead in Northern Alberta, and their unassuming wooden homes resembled the Alberta homes I remembered from my childhood.

The Russians were justifiably proud of Vostok 2 and their monument to Yuri Gagarin. He was the world's first cosmonaut to have blasted off into space on April 12, 1961. When we visited the memorial, we were given two souvenirs. One was a large heavy two-and-a-half-inch bronze commemorative medal with a picture of Yuri Gagarin on the front and the story of his flight on the back. It was nestled in a padded velvet case. Our other gift was a red leather "passport" acknowledging our visit.

No city was prouder of its subway system than Moscow. That pride was well deserved. This system was new, efficient, clean, and orderly. Each subway stop was like an art gallery with its striking wall decorations, each one unique.

On our last day in Moscow, my husband suggested we take our last subway ride.

"Let's pick the longest line and go to the very end."

When we emerged, it was a bit disappointing, nothing special to see. After we had walked around for a while, I decided to return to the hotel and pack.

"I think I'll stay and finish my roll of pictures. I've only got a few shots left and I'll never be here again. I should be back to the hotel by 5:00 PM."

Everywhere my husband traveled, he always carried his camera. It was a big bulky thing with numerous attachments, lenses and filters. When he finally pushed the shutter for his shot, it made a loud grinding sound.

Back at the hotel, I leisurely packed then sat down to read. When I glanced at my watch it was already six o'clock.

Well, Buster must have found some interesting things to photograph, I mused.

Soon it was 6:30 PM—no husband. By now I was becoming uneasy. Buster was always punctual. Seven o'clock, two hours beyond the time of his promised return; then it was 7:30 and still no husband. I sat in uneasy silence wondering what I should possibly do. By 8:00 PM, I knew I had a problem; something was wrong. I had to do something, but what? It was Saturday. The American Embassy would be closed and it would be closed tomorrow, Sunday. I knew no one in Moscow. Maybe I could find the Intourist office, but that would also be closed at this hour. The desk clerk at our hotel would be no help. If he didn't want to answer a question, he would always reply, "Niet" (no) "I don't understand."

But I had to do something. I made up my mind that I would wait until 8:30 PM, and if my husband had not returned, I would go downstairs to try to find someone who spoke English. I couldn't just sit here in helpless silence. I had to do something.

It was now 8:30. Key in hand, I started for the door when the handle turned. It was my returning husband. He was smiling.

"Oh! Where have you been?"

He put his fingers to his lips in a gesture for silence. I knew what that meant. Before our trip, we had agreed we would not discuss anything of importance inside our room because it was undoubtedly "bugged."

"Come on, Helen, let's go for a walk." As we walked along in the dark, he told me his unnerving story.

"After you left, Helen, I looked for things to photograph. Nothing was very inspiring until I saw a solid-looking square building with a date over the door. Bricks were sloughing off at the corners. I thought this would make a good photo to show the shoddiness of Russian construction, a recent building that was already deteriorating. I clicked the shutter, and out of nowhere, a hand tapped me on the shoulder. I turned to see a brawny man motioning me to follow him. I don't understand Russian, but I understood the meaning. He led me into the building, down a dark hall and into a room where the walls were thickly padded in black leather. He closed the door and left me alone. I sat in absolute silence for over half an hour, not a sound, only my heartbeat pounding in my throat.

What was this all about? Was this a jail? What had I done wrong? This must have something to do with my photographing this building. It must be some important government building, I reasoned. When the door finally opened, the brawny man returned with three other brawny men. They spoke to me in Russian. I understood not a word; they spoke among themselves, looked at me, and left. By now I sensed I was in police custody, but why? What if they wanted my film? I hurriedly took the roll out of the camera and stuffed it into my shorts.

About 6:30, the men returned. With them was a young man who spoke to me in broken English.

"I'm a student at the university and I have been asked to translate."

Then the questioning began.

"Where do you live?"

"What is your work?"

"Why are you in Moscow?"

"Who sent you here?"

"How long have you been in Moscow?"

"Where are you going next?"

"Have you ever been here before?"

"Are you here on business?"

"If you are here only as a tourist, why would a tourist want to come to Moscow?"

"Who pays for your trip?"

"Do you have enough money to pay for your own trip? Does anyone pay for your trip?"

"Why did you photograph this building?"

"Let us have your film."

Uh-oh! I thought. *What do I do now?* I opened the camera to show them there was no film.

"But this man saw you take a photograph."

"Oh," I replied, "I can understand why he might think that. But I was only looking through the lens to get a better view of the distant streets. This lens acts like a binocular."

The men examined my open camera and looked through the lens.

"Why did you want to examine this building more closely?"

"Why did you come to this spot?"

"There are no tourist sites here. What made you come here?"

The questioning continued on and on and on; the same questions over and over again. I tried to sound bewildered and dumb, a naive man willing to cooperate, just an innocent tourist, an ignorant American trying to truthfully answer every question. After an hour, the group left and I was alone with the student who eagerly began his own questioning.

"Have you ever been to Hollywood?"

"Do you know any movie stars?"

"Have you seen the movie *Mary Poppins?*"

About 7:45 PM, the men returned, spoke to the student, and he repeated their order.

"You are free to go now."

I learned that I had photographed the Russian secret police headquarters, and I guess, I am lucky they let me leave. I must have convinced them I was just an innocent harmless American tourist."

"Thank God for that," I replied. "It is frightening to imagine what might have happened. Oh, I am so glad we are leaving. Tomorrow we'll be in Poland. Things will be better there."

By the time we arrived at our little Warsaw hotel, it was late in the evening, but anxious to explore the area, we set off for a quick tour. Tired but relieved to be in a safe country, we returned to our hotel and fell soundly asleep.

The next morning, anxious to begin my morning routine, I reached for my suitcase, but it wasn't where I remembered putting it. A quick look around was fruitless.

"Buster, did you happen to move my suitcase?"

A thorough search by both of us revealed nothing. My suitcase was nowhere in that room. Slowly the horrible truth hit me. My precious suitcase had been stolen. Someone must have taken it from our locked hotel room when we'd gone for our walk the night before.

That suitcase was my lifeline. Everything I needed to survive while traveling was in that indispensable bag: medications, cosmetics, soap, shampoo, hair curlers, underwear, changes of clothing, spare shoes, my raincoat and rain boots, a warm sweater, every article carefully selected to last me for months of traveling.

All gone. Missing. I couldn't even brush my teeth.

"Buster, I have no makeup," I lamented.

"I'm sure we'll be able to find some makeup for you."

"I don't have a clean pair of panties."

"I'm sure there is a store where we can buy you some panties."

"Buster, I don't have my birth control pills."

My husband slammed his fist on the dresser.

"Damn it! We are going to the police."

We stopped at the hotel desk to report our stolen suitcase. If we had thought our Russian hotel clerk was tone deaf, that was nothing compared to this Polish hotel clerk.

"You are mistaken. Nothing has ever been stolen from our hotel guests. Never!"

He turned away and began shuffling papers.

"May we see the manager?"

The manager finally appeared, an erect, well-dressed, good-looking young man with an air of authority. He spoke no English, but I sensed he understood every word my husband and I spoke among ourselves. He refused to listen to our story. As he walked away, I understood his Polish.

"Nothing has ever been stolen or gone missing in my hotel. Don't insult my hotel."

At the Polish police station, an officer listened politely to my report in my broken Polish.

"Please wait here while I send for my sergeant. Now please repeat for him everything you have told me."

The two men took notes as I spoke.

"Pani Ivanhoe (Mrs. Ivanhoe), my sergeant will make an investigation to determine if you really did have a suitcase when you came to the hotel. Make a list of everything you had in that valise and list its value. Come back in two days, and we'll give you our report. Meantime go shopping to replace your lost items. Our stores have everything you will need."

As we trudged from shop to shop, searching for my bare necessities among the sparsely stocked shelves, my muddled mind suddenly focused.

"Buster! I know someone in this city. It's a lady I met in 1957 who is the Police pathologist for the city of Warsaw. We should see her and ask for help."

On my return trip across the Atlantic from Europe in 1957, I had boarded the ship in Lisbon, Portugal. That ship was a small unpretentious vessel, plain with no frills, but the fare was the least expensive I could find. When I entered my cabin, I saw six closely spaced bunks, four of them occupied by young college students returning home after a summer of traveling. On one bunk sat a forlorn, downcast, sad-looking middle-aged lady.

"What's wrong with her?" I asked.

"Oh, she is Polish and understands no English so no one can talk to her."

When I addressed the woman in Polish, a transformation took place and the lady blossomed. I learned that Pani Yaworska was a pathologist for the Warsaw police department. She was on her way to visit her brother in Toronto whom she had not seen since 1939. Our ship was to dock in Quebec City. Her brother had sent her a train ticket from Quebec to Toronto, Ontario. As our vessel approached the docking area, Pani Yaworska said, "I'm sort of afraid. I don't know anyone here. How will I know where to go?"

"Okay, do this," I said. "Write your brother's name and address in big print," which she did.

"When you get off the ship, hold up your train ticket and your brother's name and keep repeating "Mine brudder. Mine brudder." People will help you.

Pani Yaworska made it to Toronto. Ever since 1957, we had kept in touch, and I had her address with me.

"Why don't we go and visit my police pathologist friend," I said. "Maybe she can help us."

Pani Yaworska was surprised and pleased to see us. She made no promises but assured us the police would diligently pursue our case.

As instructed, we returned to the Warsaw police department two days after our initial visit.

"My sergeant has made an investigation and determined that you did indeed have a suitcase and that it is now missing. Your estimate of the value of the contents is $250. Go to the hotel manager and tell him he must pay you $250."

When we passed the message on to the hotel manager, he haughtily replied.

"My hotel is not paying for any suitcase you claim was stolen."

Next day, back we went to the police department.

"The manager says he isn't obliged to pay us."

"Go back to the hotel manager and tell him the Warsaw police department has determined he must pay you."

"Nobody tells me what to do," the indignant hotel manager replied when we gave him that message.

When I relayed that latest message to "our" policeman, he spoke very firmly.

"Tell the hotel manager to call me."

That latest message was the magic word. When I repeated it to the hotel manager, his attitude toward us changed.

"While you were gone, I carefully reviewed your case, and yes, we do owe you the $250, and yes, we will pay you. It will take me several days to get all the paperwork ready. When are you leaving Poland? On Tuesday, you say?" Come back on Monday and I will have all the paperwork ready for you."

Most of our vacation had been spent traipsing back and forth between the hotel and the police station, but we did have a few precious days left.

"Let's forget our problems and let's do something nice for ourselves. Let's hire a taxi and go to the park outside of Warsaw where my ancestor General Sowinski is honored with a statue to his memory."

At the center of a well-kept park, we gazed at the tall bronze statue of a proud, erect man standing on one leg. That valiant soldier had lost his leg fighting a winning battle against his Russian enemy. I proudly read my great-great-grandfather's plaque.

General Josef Longin Sowinski
1777–1831
Fallen 6 1x 1831 on the ramparts of Woli in defense of the Motherland

I think I walked away one inch taller that day, proud of my Polish heritage.

The next day we boarded a train to Cracow and visited the Auschwitz concentration camp, that haunting reminder of Nazi brutality. We walked under a sign above the entrance gate.

"Arbeit macht frei." Work makes one free.

The guide led us into a dark chamber with two massive gray ovens.

"This is the crematorium where bodies were placed into the oven and burned."

From the history of World War II, I knew what the German Gestapo had done to the various peoples they wanted to remove from society, the Poles, the Jews, the Gypsies.

But as I stared at those wide pull-out trays I could not believe that human beings could conduct such a horror on other human beings.

I felt sick. Was I imagining that I could smell the odor of burning flesh? Our visit left us both with unpleasant memories of unspeakable horrors. We were relieved to leave Auschwitz concentration camp.

We returned to "our" hotel to find that not only was our paperwork not ready, we did not have a room.

"You neglected to make a reservation." The clerk smiled.

I was sure I had made a reservation, but one can't argue with a blank wall.

Was the hotel attempting to retaliate? Angry, disappointed, and discouraged, we tried several small hotels within the area, but they were all full. In desperation, we phoned Pani Yaworska about our plight.

"You can come and stay with me," she immediately offered.

Pani Yaworska's place was tiny; her bed was a niche in the wall, her living room about the size of a lady's closet. There was a spartan bathroom but no kitchen. She shared a hot plate in the narrow hall with a neighbor. All this did not seem like a fitting residence for the police pathologist of Warsaw.

The neighbor's place was a bit larger, large enough for a couch to be opened up into a bed, with just enough space to walk around. The two ladies, Pani Yaworska and her neighbor, Anna, graciously fixed us a meal spread out on a colorful Polish tablecloth. Crusty bread with butter, juicy red tomatoes, and crunchy sliced cucumbers had never tasted better. We left the next morning with typical Polish politeness, kisses on the cheeks, bows and handshakes, and our profuse sincere thanks. The two ladies had been a godsend to us.

Before we left Warsaw, we had two important errands to run. My mother in Alberta, Canada, had promised to write, so with great hopes of a letter with news of my family, we walked to the address of the travel agency I had given her in downtown Warsaw.

As soon as we walked in, I spotted the mail collection area, and there in the slot under *I*, I could see my mother's letter, the Canadian stamp, the airmail envelope, and my mother's familiar handwriting. Two young women were standing chatting in front of the mail slots. Eager for mother's news, I walked up to the ladies.

"Excuse me please. I have come to pick up my mail. The name is Ivanhoe."

"We are closed. Come back at two o'clock," one lady replied.

"I don't mean to inconvenience you, but that's my letter right next to you, under *I*. Could you possibly reach for it and hand it to me?"

"We are closed. Come back at two o'clock."

"But please, my letter is right there."

"We are closed. Come back at two o'clock."

The absurdity of the situation—all a girl had to do was reach for my letter and hand it to me without even changing position. In a burse of indignation, I pushed open the little door separating me from the mail slots, brushed past the two women, and shouted, "That's my letter!" I grabbed it and ran.

I was gone before either of the startled ladies reacted.

Our last errand was to visit the police station and thank "our" policeman for his help in resolving our lost luggage claim.

"We have been promised payment, but the paperwork is still not completed."

"Give me your mailing address, and I'll see that you get your money."

We shook hands and left for the airport to return to Rome.

We had been in Rome a month when an official-looking letter arrived from Poland.

This letter confirms that Hotel Saskia will pay you the equivalent in zlotys of $250. You must take this letter to a Polish Embassy and have your signatures verified to acknowledge acceptance.

This money cannot be taken out of Poland. It will be paid in Polish zloty and must remain in Poland.

It was a simple matter to take the letter to the Polish Embassy in Rome for signature verification. And as for the money staying within Poland? We solved that by writing a letter, our signatures again verified by the Polish Embassy, that the full amount of the restitution was to go to Pani Yaworska. We wrote and told her to expect it. When she got it, we received a thank-you from Pani Yaworska and Anna, carefully handwritten in English.

"Thank you for the money. We hope someday to take our revenge."

Why would they say "revenge"? But when I checked the word in my dictionary, it read, "Revenge—repayment for an act."

In 1965, to the best of my knowledge, I was the first American woman to have received restitution from a Communist government.

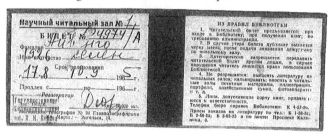

Russia Tourist "Passport"

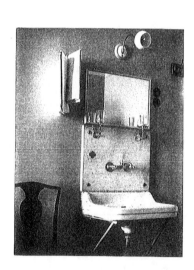

Moscow Hotel sink

Polish Visa

Chapter 4
Helen with "Beefeater" guard at Tower of London.

Travel documents

Chapter 7
International Driving Permit
International Certificate of Vaccination (The Yellow Card)
Passport

CHAPTER
5

Turkey

"How would you like to go to Turkey for a few months, Helen? Ferhan Sanlav has just phoned to ask if I am available. This will be a splendid opportunity to explore another country."

Ferhan was a very personable geologist whom we had met in California years before. We looked forward to seeing him again. This gracious man met us at the Ankara airport and drove us to the small hotel we had reserved. My husband's contract did not include lodging, so our hotel choice was a frugal one. My clearest memory of that hotel, the Hotel Barikan, is of the nauseating smell of sewer gas that rose up in the bathroom each time I turned on a tap. No matter how gently I turned a faucet, up surged that sickening smell. I couldn't win that one!

When my husband left for work the next morning, he asked me to change some American money into Turkish lira.

"I'll be working, but you'll have time to check around for the best rate."

"Go to a bank," the hotel clerk advised me. "Some people go to a bazaar where a merchant will give you a better rate, but that is illegal in Turkey."

I knew what the bank rate was, so I decided to check out the rates at the bazaar. I wandered around until I found a cloth merchant with no customers nearby.

"How much lira do you give to one American dollar?"

He glanced about, saw that there was no one close by, and whispered, "How much you want to exchange?"

"One hundred dollars."

He whispered me his rate. It was much higher than at a bank.

"Okay," I replied. "I'll exchange."

"You wait there." He motioned across the alley.

A few moments later he returned, glanced around, saw no one, took my $100, and handed me a pocket of lira.

"I'm an honest man. It's all there."

As soon as I could find a quiet corner, I counted my lira. The merchant had given me too much lira, far too much. What should I do? Keep it or return it? I wanted to be able to exchange money in the future so I decided on the honest approach—go back and tell him he'd given me too many lira.

But as I approached the merchant, he turned away.

"Sorry, madam. I am very busy."

"You made a mistake," I whispered.

"Madam, I am an honest man."

"Yes, you are an honest man, and I am an honest woman. You gave me too much money."

I handed the packet of lira back to him. As he began to count, his eyes got bigger, his mouth dropped open, and a look of complete shock enveloped his face. He looked at me with incredulity.

"Oh! Madam! Thank you! Thank you!"

He shook my hand vigorously.

"Madam, you take tea? Take tea, madam?"

I visited him many times during our stay and was always greeted with "Take tea, madam? Take tea?"

The Turkish merchants wanted the American dollars. When an American geologist friend asked me if I would trade in his dollars at the market to get the more advantageous exchange of Turkish lira, I had no trouble doing so. But what would have happened to me if the authorities had caught me breaking the law?

Walking around Ankara, I was convinced that the taxi driver's aim in life was to see how many pedestrians they could run over. As I ran across the wide streets, I was positive they accelerated when they saw me. Riding in a taxi one day, I called out to the driver.

"You just went through a red light."

"Oh, yes," he replied. "Some lights are red, some are yellow, and some are green."

On downtown Ankara streets, a loud cry of "Ulus! Ulus! Ulus!" would rise about the traffic din. I saw a small van packed with people and a young boy clinging to the outside, shouting, "Ulus! Ulus! Ulus!"

"What does that mean?" I asked a well-dressed young woman.

"Oh, that is a group taxi going to an area called Ulus. It's much cheaper than a regular taxi, and we all ride them."

From then on, I always looked for those less expensive group taxis and stayed away from the red light runners.

There was a smell to Ankara, not an unpleasant smell but a strong smell, one I finally recognized. It was the smell of mutton. Big, fat sheep carcasses hung in butcher shop windows, each one decorated with a huge red paper rose thrust between the two hind quarters. Eye catching, to say the least. Every household in Ankara must be cooking mutton every day. I could smell mutton everywhere—on my clothes, in my hair, and even in the bedsheets.

Wherever there were pedestrians on the busy streets in Ankara, there were shoeshine boys with their shiny polished brass shoeshine kits calling out for customers. I approached a clean-looking young man.

"Shine, madame?"

He pulled up a low stool, and I sat down. All around us the other shoeshine boys began laughingly calling out to him in Turkish. I was sure the laughter was directed at me. I was glad I couldn't understand Turkish. The young shoeshine lad pretended not to hear and proceeded to give my shoes the highest, glossiest polish possible.

I watched as an older man wearing rumpled clothes approached a shoeshine boy. His boots were leather but cracked, old, ripped, and muddy. He seemed unsure of himself. He spoke to the boy, pointing to his shoes. The shoeshine boy looked at the grubby shoes, laughed, and shook his head. The rumpled man walked to another shoeshine boy and received the same reaction, laughter and a shake of the head. His shoulders slumped as he walked away, a picture of dejection. I felt sorry for him.

Ferhan Sanlav phoned us one Friday evening.

"A group of students from the Ankara University are going on an overnight trip this weekend to a very interesting place in Cappadocia. It's a unique geological area where people lived in caves and where there is a wealth of Christian history. If there is space on the bus, would you be interested in joining the students?"

Of course we agreed. Ferhan phoned us back.

"You are in luck. There is space on the bus. You can pay your fare tomorrow when you get on the bus. Overnight accommodation is included. Oh, and Helen, please be understanding about your room."

At the bus we were greeted by an enthusiastic group of lively young men and women in a holiday mood, all of them outgoing and exuberant, laughing and talking in Turkish and English.

"You are our honored guests, Mr. and Mrs. Ivanhoe. We have reserved these two front seats for you."

The good nature of the young people was infectious, and time passed quickly. Whenever we passed a small village, the students chorused out, "Chai! Chai! Tea! Tea!" The obliging driver complied, and the young people eagerly bounded out for a flavorful cup of Turkish tea.

As we drove along an agreeable young man acted as our self-appointed guide, explaining the topography to us.

"What you see in the far distance are volcanic cones, but you are in for a surprise. You will soon see the result of millions of years of ancient volcanic eruptions."

Surprised and delighted, we saw ahead of us numerous high cone-shaped and dome-shaped structures.

"These are the famous tufa stone caves of Cappadocia."

As soon as we got off the bus, our gracious guide led us from cave to cave.

"Tufa stone is soft, compressed volcanic ash, so people easily dug out these domes to make homes. In these caves centuries ago, Christians hid from prosecution. This cave is where Saint Barbara lived. And look at the paintings on the walls of their homes—religious symbols, fruits, apples, plants, all brightly colored."

Fascinated we wandered among the caves. A young boy furtively approached me.

"Madam! Madam!" he whispered.

In his hand, he held what appeared to be a bronze, corroded Byzantine cross about four inches high.

"Madam! You buy?"

"How much?"

The boy glanced around nervously.

"Five American dollars," in a barely audible voice.

I paid him. He handed me the cross and was gone in an instant. Had I unknowingly bought stolen goods?

Today, that cross, beautifully framed, hangs on our living room wall. Is it authentic or a well-made replica?

When we arrived at our hotel that evening, I understood why Ferhan had asked us to be understanding about our room. It had a bed. That was it—just a bed and two small hand towels. Sanitary facilities were outside, a tap with running water and a toilet that was a hole in a marble slab.

Now I knew what a "Turkish toilet" was.

That evening we gathered in a big plain restaurant for supper. My husband and I had come to admire Turkish food, always flavorful and satisfying, always a wide variety of choices, always nicely served. Was this a heritage passed down from the Ottoman sultans?

Buster and I ordered frugally, not sure of the prices. But the young man sitting next to us ordered item after item, soup, salad, two breads, two stews, rice, and several desserts.

He must be well-off, I mused.

Then came our bill. It had been totaled to include everything anyone had ordered, then divided by the number of people eating, so every diner paid the same amount.

No wonder the young man had ordered with such abandon. He knew something we did not. He knew that all the rest of us would be paying for his extravagant meal.

The next day on the long drive across the Anatolian plain, back to Ankara, the students never lost their exuberant good nature. It must have been the result of the numerous cups of chai, that delicious Turkish tea they kept consuming.

We were in Izmir on the Aegean Sea coast where my husband had gone to meet with a Dutch geologist. The geologist took us to see a belly dancing show, where the dancers were all older, heavy middle-aged women. I wondered what kind of future these unfortunate ladies would have in a Muslim country.

"Let's have an adventure," my husband announced. "For our return trip from Izmir to Ankara, let's go by local bus so we can see the countryside and learn more about Turkey."

We found the bus depot, bought our ticket, $5.50 each, and were told to arrive promptly at 8:00 AM.

"Is this a first-class bus?" I asked.

"Oh sure, madame, first class," the agent replied, and he laughed. That should have been my first clue.

"What time does the bus arrive in Ankara?" I asked.

"The schedule says 4:00 PM, but that's only a guess," he replied, again with laughter.

That should have been my second clue.

We arrived at the bus depot the next morning well before 8:00 AM, saw two empty places at the very front of the bus, and pleased with our unrestricted view sat down on the wooden seats. A first-class bus with wooden seats? The bus rapidly filled with passengers, people of all ages, but mostly men. When the driver got on, he spoke to us in Turkish. We didn't understand, he gestured, tried speaking again, this time more loudly, becoming very frustrated at our lack of comprehension. Finally a young man volunteered.

"Old people this seat. You move."

We ended up sitting near the back of the bus. Promptly at 8:00 AM, the bus lurched ahead, the top of the vehicle piled so high with baggage, bags and boxes that I wondered if we were top heavy. My husband opened up a map for us to follow our progress, which so far appeared to be a slow speed of a maximum twenty miles per hour. The driver had a helper, a nice-looking young boy who sat beside him. Frequently the driver would run his big hands across the lad's back, occasionally slipping his hand under the lad's T-shirt. It made me uncomfortable to watch, so I would turn away. As soon as we were away from the city, the helper turned on the music, an unfamiliar, loud minor-key Oriental sound that monotonously blared on and on and on. To me, it was exceedingly unpleasant.

Try to shut it out. Try to think of something else, I told myself.

"Think of stories and fables from Turkey. Think of the story of King Midas with the golden touch."

King Midas was the king of Phrygia, an ancient kingdom in Turkey. Midas had been kind to the gods, so they gave him his choice of a reward. Midas asked that everything he touched would be turned to gold. But alas! He touched his beautiful beloved young daughter, and she immediately turned to gold. His food and drink turned to gold, and he begged the gods to take back their gift. The gods promised that if Midas bathed in a sacred river, he would lose his "golden touch." Thereafter the sands of that river have contained the gold washed off King Midas.

Turkish fables gave us the Gordian knot story. At one time, the Phrygians were without a king. The gods declared that the next man to enter the city driving an oxcart would be king. A peasant farmer named Gordias drove into town in an oxcart and was immediately declared king by the gods. His son, Midas of the Golden Touch, showed his gratitude to the gods by taking the oxcart into his palace and tying it to a post with an intricate knot called the Gordian knot. Over the centuries, no one could undo this perplexing Gordian knot until Alexander the Great, in 333 BC, sliced it in half with one blow of his mighty sword.

From the Phrygian kingdom of 1200 BC to our present century is a long time, but we still refer to a soft conical cap with the top pulled forward as the Phrygian cap. This cap, still worn today, is said to signify freedom and the pursuit of happiness. Wouldn't it be nice if we could all have one?

How many of us would have known that Aesop's fables came down the ages from Turkey? Aesop was a Phrygian slave. Many ancient kingdoms lay claim to his actual birthplace, but all respect Aesop as the teller of those moralizing animal stories we heard as small children.

Before the Phrygians, the dominant peoples of the Anatolian plain were the Hittites. The capital city of this powerful empire covered four hundred acres fortified by a massive wall over four miles in length. The Hittites intrigued me because they wore shoes with turned up toes, and when I read that the Etruscans of Italy wore the same type of shoe, I wondered if there was a tie between these two ancient peoples. Legend says the Hittites had a crack troop of women warriors called the Amazons. Fact or fiction?

It was a fact that as I tried hard to concentrate on tales of Turkey, the monotonous, exotic music was momentarily less intrusive. It was fun to recall tales of Troy, that ancient city on the coast of the Aegean Sea. Troy controlled traffic through the Dardanelles between Asia and Europe and had been occupied for over three thousand five hundred years. During those centuries, there had been many Troys, each built on top of the debris of the previous city, each becoming powerful because of its strategic location. Was the Trojan War of 1200 BC to recapture Helen stolen from Troy by the Greeks? Or was it to regain control of trade through the Dardanelles?

Agamemnon led the Greeks in the Trojan War to recover Helen. He sacrificed his lovely young daughter Iphigenia to appease the winds before he sailed against Troy. After the defeat of Troy, Agamemnon returned to Greece but was slain by his wife, Clytemnestra, and her lover. Two of Agamemnon's children then avenged his death by slaying the wife and her lover. A true Greek tragedy, the story of a useless war.

Of all the Turkish tales, my favorite is of the man who rode his donkey sitting backward. When asked why he rode in this position, he gave this logical response.

"I will see where I am going soon enough. I want to look behind me to see where I have been to help me remember what I have seen."

We drove across a flat plain, stopping at small villages, some of which were only a police station and a few houses, but there was always a tiny school. Ataturk had decreed that every child must learn to read and write.

When he became the first president of the Turkish republic in 1923, Kemal Mustafa Ataturk, an exceptional leader encouraged the adoption of a constitution to modernize Turkey. Freedom of thought, of speech, and of the press were guaranteed. The changes Ataturk brought to Turkey were dramatic. Polygamy was outlawed. The wearing of the Turkish fez was forbidden. The Gregorian calendar was adopted. The difficult Arab script was replaced by the Latin alphabet. All religious education was removed from the schools. Ataturk believed that education would eliminate the inequalities that existed among the Turks. No longer would the literate few dominate the illiterate majority. Schools were built by the thousands across Turkey, and now, about forty years later, we could observe that his legacy still stood.

Ataturk had been a remarkable leader who gave the Turkish people a national pride. Surrounded by the incessant never-ending beat of the loud unfamiliar, minor-key Eastern music, I wished Ataturk had advocated the playing of Western music on all long-distance buses.

My head ached, my body ached, the wooden seat was becoming increasingly uncomfortable, and it was becoming hot. I pointed to our map.

"It is one o'clock. If we are to be in Ankara by four o'clock, we should be halfway by now, and we aren't nearly that far. And I can't tolerate this music."

Just then the music stopped, the bus stopped, and the passengers began piling out.

"This must be a lunch stop. Let's join the crowd," my husband sighed.

The lunch stop was clean and cooler but how to order from a menu where you understand nothing? The waiter sensed our dilemma, motioned for us to follow him, and led us into the kitchen where savory smells bubbled up from huge copper pots. In sign language, the waiter indicated we should point to our selection. We chose a bubbling stew of vegetables and meat. Buster and I agreed that the meal we had selected was one of the most delicious of our Turkish stay.

Back to the hard seats. Back to the loud music. After we had all taken our seats, the young helper started down the aisle with a big jar of pink liquid, stopping by each passenger and pouring a small amount into the person's palm. People then splashed the liquid onto their faces.

"Rose water," my husband guessed. It did feel refreshing. By four o'clock, I wondered how much longer before this trip would finally be over.

"Oh, I am so hot and uncomfortable and my head hurts," I lamented. "And that loud music!"

"Helen!" my husband spoke sharply. "For the first time in our married life, you are starting to complain and I don't like it. Stop! Stop it!"

No sympathy there. Hour after slow hour, the bus rumbled on, only the hourly dispensing of the rose water broke the monotony. Occasionally in the flat distance we could spot a huge earth mound. We wondered if these could be tels, remains of some ancient city on the Anatolian plain. Names came to mind, the Hurrians, the Mittani, the Cimmerian horsemen who crafted remarkable gold ornaments, the Lydians who invented dice and the first coinage, the Urartians who discovered metallurgy, but we lacked a sufficient knowledge of Turkish history to place these ancient peoples in a chronological or geographic order. I made myself a pledge to learn more of this country's ancient past when we got off this uncomfortable bus. Six o'clock, seven o'clock, then in the far, far distance, a slight glow, surely that must finally be Ankara. By 8:30, we thankfully entered the city, yet it was almost 9:00 in the evening before we disembarked at the bus depot.

"Thank God! Thank God! We are finally here. What a long, long day."

"Look at it this way, Helen. Where else in the world could you ride a bus for thirteen hours for only five and one-half dollars?"

"Ferhan has no more work for me, but before we leave Turkey, we must visit Istanbul. There are buses daily from Ankara to Istanbul, so let's pick a day and go. I promise there will be no Oriental music."

In Istanbul we found a small clean inexpensive hotel, but that night we were severely bitten by some unknown critters.

"Bus, we have to move. My body is covered in red welts."

We moved to another small inexpensive hotel. It was noisy but fortunately devoid of unknown critters.

To be a tourist in Istanbul is to stand in the middle of centuries of history, almost too overwhelming to logically comprehend.

Three names, three walls. First it was called Byzantium surrounded by a high wall; then it became Constantinople, capital of the East Roman Empire, surrounded by two more thick, high impregnable stone walls. Those walls were breached in 1453 when the Ottoman Turks laid siege to Constantinople, and Istanbul became the new capitol of Turkey.

Where to start? How best to see this fascinating city?

We walked and we walked. We walked across the Galata Bridge, stopping to savor the freshly caught tiny fish that a young boy was selling from his sizzling pan of bubbling oil. It was delicious, guts and all. We signed up for tours of the palaces, staring at the treasures and incredibly lavish furnishings—not just one palace but many, each more lavish than the last. Where did the Ottoman sultans get all this wealth?

We gazed at ancient Roman ruins, those massive forgotten underground cisterns rediscovered in modern times. We marveled at delicate Byzantine mosaics and gazed in admiration at the stunningly decorated revered mosques.

My memory grows fuzzy with the passage of decades. Was that beautiful ceiling I would never forget in the Blue Mosque or was it in the Suleiman Mosque?

But one tableau remains clearly etched in my memory, sharp and painful as the day I first observed it. I had been walking atop the thick wide walls surrounding Istanbul when I heard a child's scream, a loud piercing scream like nothing I had ever heard before. It was a scream coming from agony and intense pain. I turned to see a mother running toward a small child. She wrapped her arms around the little girl, but the shrill screaming continued. The mother picked up the child, hoisted her onto her back, and bounced the youngster back and forth. The helpless, hopeless face of the mother, the incessant shrill, strident screams of the little girl in obvious pain—and there was nothing I could do. A helpless feeling and sympathy I could not even express to the mother. A boy, about ten years old, was sitting cross-legged on the ground, laboriously cutting old tires into strips. He looked up, listless and resigned. There was nothing he could do either—it was as if he had seen this all before.

I walked away, but the agony of that child haunts me still.

IZMIR
Helen with Turkish teapot.

IZMIR
Loading bus for trip to Ankara.

Chapter
5
Turkey

GOREME ancient church
in a cave.

GOREME - Helen exiting
ancient church

Village lady

Village children

Ancient churchyard

Pergumum Ancient
Roman Amphitheatre

PERGE
Where St. Paul
preached

CHAPTER

6

California Calls

A name like "Pensione Texas" in the center of Rome is sure to attract attention. Our first experience in that pleasant pensione had been so enjoyable that we chose it once more for a short stay. We had decided it was time to return to California. Our daughter, Cheryl, had been enrolled at California Lutheran College, and we were anxious to see how she had survived her parents' year-long absence. (She had managed very well.)

"First I have to let my clients know my schedule," my geologist husband announced.

"Zvi Alexander wants me to stop in Tel Aviv to discuss a proposed venture and Occidental Petroleum (Oxy) has asked me to check on a matter in Cairo."

To fly from Rome to Tel Aviv was no problem, but how to get to Cairo, a Muslim country, from Jewish Israel?

Any time my husband and I had arrived at Lod Airport in Tel Aviv, our request to immigration had been a polite petition.

"Please don't stamp my passport."

Immigration always obliged, knowing that we might be visiting Muslim countries and wanted no record of having been in Israel. The usual way of entry to Egypt from Israel was via Cyprus, so that became our plan.

As soon as our plane arrived in Nicosia, Cyprus, we headed directly to the Traveler's Aid desk to inquire about a room.

"Oh, dear! We are so sorry. All our hotels are booked. The United Nations is here on a peacekeeping mission between Greece and Turkey. Sorry! We cannot help you."

"Are you sure?" I pleaded. "Can't you find us something?"

"Well, I do see we have a newer hotel on the outskirts of town. But it is so new that it has not yet been rated so I can't tell you much about it. Do you want me to call and see if they have rooms?"

"Please."

"You are in luck. They do have a room, but it has no private bath. Shall I book it for you?"

"We don't have much choice," Buster responded. "We'll take it."

The taxi delivered us to a brightly lit, clean hotel. Near the reception desk, there was an attractive lobby where several very pretty young girls sat in comfortable lounge chairs.

The hotel had no elevator. As we turned to walk up the stairs, we saw a young man standing at the foot of the stairway, his eyes constantly surveying the nearby rooms, almost as if he were a sentry on duty.

When we came back downstairs and sat down in the dining room, I heard an American lady's voice at a table near to us say to her male companion, probably her husband, "Oh, I'm sure they are."

At another table an American officer stood up and shook the hand of his dinner companion, a very beautiful petite young woman. He bowed and kissed the lady's hand, turned, and walked to the exit.

The "sentry" stepped aside, and the pretty woman walked upstairs.

As I looked around the cheerful dining room, I saw several young soldiers wearing UN emblems sitting at tables with seductively dressed pretty young girls, sipping wine, smiling, and chatting.

"Well, Helen. What do you think?"

"I think we are about to experience a night in a high class brothel."

The bed was very comfortable; the night was quiet, and we slept very well.

The next morning, I set out to explore Nicosia. In the center of town was a no-man's land, patrolled by UN soldiers, Greeks on one side of a fence barricade, Turks on the other side of the barricade, between them a dry, bleak, barren stretch of dirt where windblown papers rolled along amid the dust. The people on the Greek side glared silently at the people on the Turkish side, and the people on the Turkish side glared silently at the people on the Greek side.

A Greek Cypriot told me his story.

"We were peaceful people, living peacefully when we were invaded by the Turks."

A Turkish Cypriot told me a different story.

"Turkey was forced to move into Cyprus to protect my fellow Turks."

Another invasion added to the long history of ancient Cyprus. Phoenicians, Assyrians, Egyptians, Persians, Arabs, Crusaders, Turks, British, and Greeks all fought over this strategically located tiny island. Would real peace ever come to the Cypriots?

Buster wanted to look up a geologist friend who had retired in the port town of Limassol. While my husband was off to discuss geology with his friend, I decided to don my blue Israeli bikini and sun tan on a quiet, uncrowded wharf near our hotel. No sooner had I spread my towel and lay down in the warm sun when a teenage boy appeared and intently stared at me.

"Oh, go away," I muttered.

He did go away, but moments later, he reappeared with a dozen more teenage boys, all of whom surrounded me, silently staring, their gaping mouths open in amazement.

I grabbed my towel and rushed back to the hotel.

Was I the first female body these boys had ever seen?

Occidental Petroleum had made us a paid reservation at the Hilton Hotel in Cairo. We stepped into a brightly decorated lobby. An orchestra was playing, couples were dancing, people were laughing and drinking. Everyone was elegantly dressed. Then I spotted a beautiful bride in a sensational sequined gown, bedecked in gold jewelry, scintillating under the lights. I had never seen so much gold on a lady.

"What is going on?" I asked the bellboy.

"Oh, this is the wedding of a Saudi prince. They like to come to Cairo for the wedding because they can drink alcohol here. Of course, you know alcohol is forbidden in Saudi."

When Buster stepped up to the desk to register, the clerk shook his head.

"No. We have no reservation for a Mr. and Mrs. Ivanhoe."

At first Buster politely asked for the clerk to check again.

"No. Nothing for you."

In a loud commanding voice, Buster called out.

"Let me see the manager."

The manager hurried over.

"Sir!" Buster announced. "I am here representing a major oil company, Occidental Petroleum Corporation. I demand you honor their request for a room."

A hurried conversation between the manager and the desk clerk, shuffling of papers, and more whispered conversations, then the manager announced, "Yes, Mr. and Mrs. Ivanhoe, we can accommodate you, and we apologize for the misunderstanding. The bellboy will see you to your room."

We stepped inside our spacious quarters with an unobstructed view of the Nile River. I saw a huge bouquet of red roses on a dresser. A gigantic basket of fruit enveloped in saran wrap and tied with a wide red ribbon covered the coffee table.

What a great welcome, I thought.

But the roses and the fruit basket were hastily gathered up and quickly whisked away before I could say a word.

"Uh-oh! We got someone else's room." My husband smiled. "Someone important had been scheduled to stay here."

I often wondered where those unfortunate people we had displaced slept that night.

Buster went off to take care of his business, and I had the day free to spend in the Cairo Museum. Amazed, overwhelmed, and awed by the displays of antiquity, the museum's closing came all too soon. And I had seen only a small fraction of this marvelous museum.

That evening, Buster was handed a cable.

"Guess what, Helen. Ferhan Sanlov wants me to come back to Ankara on a job. That means you will have to continue on to California by yourself."

The next morning, Buster surprised me with his announcement.

"I've been thinking, Helen. You have to return to California, but instead of flying west across the Atlantic, why not fly east to the Orient? You could visit the major capitals that I stopped at last year and see a whole new world."

And so began my memorable around-the-world adventure.

Around the World in Thirty Days

We sat down to discuss my trip.

"It would be logical for you to fly to Tehran, then on to New Delhi, Bangkok, Manila, Hong Kong, Tokyo, and end up in Vancouver. You can have a rest there with your sister, Valeria, before ending up in Beverly Hills."

"I'll give you a list of the hotels where I stayed in each city on my trip a year ago. When you are in Bangkok, I have a job for you. I'll give you the name, address, and phone number of the minister of petroleum. He has a map I need that he did not want to give me. Make an appointment to see him. Dress carefully and wear any good jewelry you have. Take a taxi. Don't go by bus.

"Ask for this map, number 2092. When he shows it to you immediately take it to the window and trace it. I'll give you tracing paper and draw you a map of his office showing where the window is located. Don't hesitate. Act positive and sure of yourself. Just make sure you copy the map."

We went to buy my airline ticket, an eighteen-inch accordion-pleated packet. I bought $500 worth of traveler's checks in $20 denominations.

No credit cards were available to me in 1965, but I did have a "letter of credit" from the Bank of America in Beverly Hills to use in case of necessity.

We bought a lightweight suitcase, packed with a minimal amount of clothing and my one good suit.

"Nobody sees you day after day, so no one knows you are wearing the same clothes each day. You'll be carrying your own luggage much of the time, so keep it lightweight."

Buster showed his concern when he said, "You'd be all alone on this trip and I'll be in Turkey, so you won't be able to contact me. I do know a geologist in Manila. I'll cable him and ask if you can call on him in case of emergency. Do you remember Bill Merrill?"

Indeed I did remember Bill Merrill. We were living in Bakersfield, California, in 1954 when there was a knock at our back door. I opened it to see a stranger.

"I'm Bill Merrill. Is Buster home? I need to talk to him."

There was urgency in his voice. When Buster came to the door, Bill Merrill spoke to him in an anxious tone.

"Bus, someone broke the lock on our seismic trailer and sticks of dynamite are missing. We are doing seismic work along the Kern River and had our trailer packed with supplies. I've talked to several young boys and they told me Roddy Ivanhoe was passing out sticks of dynamite."

"Oh no, Bill. Roddy wouldn't do anything like that. Not my son. No, not Roddy."

Bill Merrill left. Ten minutes later, the phone rang.

"I'm at the firehouse across the street. Tell Bus to come over immediately and bring his son with him. The fire captain wants to see him."

It turned out that Roddy had broken into the trailer packed with sticks of dynamite. He had loaded his arms with the dynamite and began passing out the sticks to any and all of his young friends.

"Here. Beat on this and see what happens."

By the grace of God, no one had been hurt, but a shocked father had to accept that his son lacked discretion and good judgment.

Yes, I remembered Bill Merrill.

Together, Bus and I took the airport bus from the Hilton to the Cairo airport.

"You may get lonely at times, so don't be afraid to talk to people. No one is going to rape you because rape isn't any fun. Don't go out after dark. Keep your passport, ticket, and money in that wallet under your belt. Keep your eyes open. Avoid unpopulated areas. You'll do fine."

As Buster turned and walked toward his Turkish airline and I continued on toward my airline, my tooth began to ache. That tooth had bothered me earlier in Rome, so while we were in Israel, I made a hurried trip to an Israeli dentist.

"It's nothing to worry about. Just keep taking aspirin," he replied casually.

My reaction to the dentist was that he couldn't care less and was much too busy to take care of a foreigner.

At the airline check-in counter, several clerks looked over my long ticket.

"May we see your yellow card?"

In 1965 international travelers were required to carry a yellow card showing which shots and immunizations that traveler had received.

The clerks called over a uniformed person, perhaps the manager.

"Madam, you have no cholera shot listed on your yellow card. Have you ever had a cholera shot?"

"No."

"Then you need a cholera shot. Where you are going you must have a cholera shot."

"What do I do?"

"We can give you a cholera shot here at the airport if you wish."

I agreed. The uniformed man led me into a nearby room where I saw two motherly looking women sitting and knitting. One woman held a small child on her lap.

"Madam needs a cholera shot."

The two women put down their knitting and placed the small child on a chair. They walked to a sink and scrubbed their hands and arms, then walked to a refrigerator, and took out a vial. They rubbed my upper arm with alcohol, then effectively administered my cholera shot.

"Would madam please sit here quietly for a few minutes?"

My arm never hurt nor did I ever have any adverse reaction to my cholera shot.

Tehran, Iran

I was entering an ancient land, a land where prehistoric man roamed this Iranian plateau thousands of years before recorded history. Here wild animals had been domesticated and grains cultivated five to eight thousand years before Christ. In antiquity, sun worshippers told fables of eternal jets of flames, arising from the escaping gases and oils of the underground petroleum deposits.

This was Persia, the land of Cyrus and Cambysis, of Darius and Xerxes, the rulers who built the magnificent outstanding city of Persepolis that stood in monumental glory until Alexander the Great destroyed it in 331 BC. History records that when Alexander carried off the loot of Persepolis before he burned the city, it took ten thousand pairs of mules and five thousand camels to haul away the spoils; so wealthy had the city been.

Eager to see the Iran of today, I looked forward to my short visit.

When I landed at the airport of Tehran, I was politely ushered through customs and immigration. After I gave the taxi driver the hotel name Buster had given me, he answered, "Yes, madam."

He opened the taxi door for me and said, "Welcome to Tehran."

I had three days to spend in Tehran. The first day I would take an extensive city tour. The second day I would walk, sightseeing along the main streets, and the third day I would spend visiting museums.

The city tour took me to the outskirts of Tehran where women were washing rugs. Those expensive Persian rugs were immersed in a stream, soaped, beaten, then spread out on the rocks to dry. Such casual treatment for such a costly article, I thought. But I was told by our guide, "This is how it has always been done."

The jewel collection at the Tehran museum was mind-boggling, that there could be so many diamonds, emeralds, rubies, sapphires, precious and semiprecious stones all in one place was almost too overwhelming to absorb. On display were elaborate jewelry, necklaces, crowns, and decorative articles covered completely in diamonds. There were cups, glasses, and serving vessels enveloped in rubies and blue sapphires. A large globe of the world where each continent was identified by a different gem made an impressive impact on a viewer. It was almost as if an artist had been given an assignment.

"Here are the gems. Do something unique with them."

And near the exit of the museum, dinner plates were lined up, heaped high with diamonds and rubies—almost like leftovers with no place to go.

From the magical world of gems, I stepped into the restroom, the WC (water closet), and there it was—a hole in the floor.

With all the wealth in this museum, why can't they put in a proper toilet? I thought.

That night my tooth throbbed and I slept very little.

Tired but eager to see India, the land that had been called "the jewel in the crown" of Great Britain, I left Tehran with a favorable impression. The people looked healthy, tall, and statuesque. Everyone had treated me with courtesy and politeness.

New Delhi, India

This must be what hell is like, I thought as I walked a Delhi street early in the morning, enveloped in a smoky haze, my visibility limited, the air filled with the sound of buzzing insects. The air was thick with the constant, incessant, never-ending droning of unseen, low, pulsating, humming life all around me. It was a sonorosity from which there was no escape. I felt trapped in a world of continuous, immutable sound.

My tooth ached. It was cold and I did not have a warm coat. Gradually the haze lifted. I walked past families living in the street, huddled by a small fire. From their cooking pots, mothers were feeding small children. Everyone looked cold and miserable. I swallowed an aspirin tablet and tried to forget about my throbbing tooth and hurried on.

A moment of panic overcame me when I saw numerous big red blobs of spittle on the sidewalk ahead of me and under my feet.

"Oh, my god! They all have TB. This must be blood spat out as a result of tuberculosis."

It took me a moment to remember what I had read. The Indians chewed a mildly narcotic nut, and this must be the saliva they spat out as they chewed. To my intense relief, I realized these red blobs were not TB, merely spit.

In the center of a busy street, a big white cow with long slender horns was lying peacefully in the middle of traffic.

Oh! This is what I have read about. I need to take a photo, I thought.

Just as I was focusing, a motorbike came up behind me, stopped with a grinding sound, and two young Indian men approached me, walking purposely.

"Why are you photographing that cow?" one of the men demanded. His voice was accusative and he looked angry.

Oh god! What do I do now? I had to think of some logical reason for taking a photo.

"Oh, my father is a farmer in Alberta, Canada, and he raises Hereford cows. This cow is so different from anything on his farm that I wanted a picture to send him."

The two men immediately relaxed and spoke kindly to me.

"How long have you been in Delhi?"

"I arrived last night. This is my first day here."

"Would you like us to drive you around and show you our city?"

"That would be wonderful."

"Hop on behind me."

And off we three went, past crowded shopping areas, down narrow lanes, alongside small parks, often stopping in front of beautiful temples for a better view.

We came to a halt before a huge red temple where small children were sitting and standing on the long steps in begging positions.

"See that boy with his broken arm hanging down? His arm was broken at birth so that he would make a more emotional appeal as a beggar. But such vile acts are outlawed in Indian today. Don't give him any money. It only encourages more of the same."

The two men drove me around for several hours, proudly pointing out buildings of note and statues of Indian gods and heroes. When I offered to pay for their gas, they politely refused.

"Just send us copies of some of the pictures you took today when you get back to America."

When we shook hands and said good-bye, I felt that I had been an honored guest in Delhi, the guest of two polite and gracious young men.

Not far from my hotel, I had noticed a clothing store. Maybe I could find a warm coat. Just as I entered, a young man broke away from a cluster of salesmen and rushed toward me. I heard him say, "This one is *my* goldfish."

Unfortunately, much as I needed a warm coat, I could not find one to fit. His goldfish had not produced.

From the hotel desk clerk I found out where I could buy a bottle of whisky, hoping that would help me sleep and dull my toothache pain. It didn't. All I got was a bleary head in the morning, but off I went on my scheduled city tour. So many things now looked familiar, thanks to yesterday's motorbike guides.

Sitting next to me on the bus was a nice-looking young Indian man.

"I see you are taking aspirin. Do you have a problem?"

"I have a toothache that comes and goes."

We chatted during the tour and exchanged pleasantries.

That night I was unable to sleep and had just fallen asleep about 11:30 when the phone rang.

"I am the man you met on the bus. I have been so worried about your toothache that I picked up a prescription for you. May I come up and bring it to you?"

I wanted to scream out, "Jesus! I finally fell asleep and you woke me up!"

Instead I said, "Leave it at the desk."

"Oh, madam. This is a complicated medicine. I must come up and explain to you how it is to be administered. It is guaranteed to cure your toothache. May I come and show you?"

"Just leave it at the desk."

He continued to be very insistent but finally realized there was no hope to seduce this American visitor, clever as his approach had been.

A day's drive to Agra to see the Taj Mahal and the Red Fort was high on my list. Would it look as beautiful as the photos I had seen? I knew that Shah Jahan, a Mogul ruler, had built the Taj Mahal as a sepulcher for Mumtaz Mahal, his beloved empress who had born him fourteen children in eighteen years.

A small group of us tourists boarded the bus in Delhi early on a cold morning. But when we settled into the bus, it was even colder.

"For heaven's sake! The air conditioner is on."

"Please, please, turn off the air conditioner," we all called out.

"I can't," the young driver replied. "I do not know how."

The flustered young man pulled and pushed buttons and levers but all to no avail. We all sat huddled over, our arms wrapped around ourselves as the cold air blasted us all the way to Agra.

We stepped from the cold bus into the warm sunshine and gasped at the building in front of us. Speechless, I stared at the marble mausoleum, a building of incredible beauty at the end of a long clear reflecting pool. The white marble mausoleum walls were inlaid with semiprecious stones in designs of beauty, delicacy and superb quality. Beautiful gardens surrounded the glittering Taj and the long pool. The Taj was indeed more beautiful than any pictures I had ever seen. It was truly one of the world's most impressive man-made structures.

Then I learned the sad ending to the life of the builder of the Taj Mahal. When Shah Jahan became ill, his sons fought over who should be his successor. To ensure there would be no interference from their father, they placed him under house arrest in the nearby Agra fort. One of his daughters tended to her ill father, and when he died, she had him interred in the Taj next to Mumtaz, his beloved wife. And there, since 1631, Shah Jahan and Mumtaz Mahal lie side by side in eternity.

"Don't drink the water and keep your fingers away from your eyes," advice given to me by my doctor when I first began traveling abroad. "Watch out for pickpockets and hang on to your purse." More good advice from a traveling friend; advice I heeded as I walked about in New Delhi. Around me there were so many pathetically poor people and so much poverty. Contrasted with the poor were the elegant Indian ladies, beautifully groomed and dressed in colorful silk saris, their faces lovely and unlined, pictures of perfect beauty. Why was there wealth yet so much poverty?

"It's the fault of the British. The British kept us subjugated for so many years and we never had a chance. It's the fault of the British."

I heard a similar statement many times and thought, *Okay, the British are gone. Now it's up to you.*

A well-dressed young Indian man spoke to me.

"Are you American?"

"Yes."

"Don't tell me. Let me guess. You are from California."

"Yes."

"Is it true that Ronald Reagan is going to run for governor of your state?"

"Yes."

"Symptom of a sick society if a Hollywood actor is picked to be governor of a state."

Thinking of the mutilated beggars and the families living in the streets, I thought, *You shouldn't talk about my country as a sick society. Look around you.*

At the airport, leaving Delhi was as time-consuming as entry into the country had been. When I entered India, I was handed a sheaf of papers to fill out. Now I was handed a similar sheaf of papers to fill out before I could leave India.

"Where are you going? How long will you be there? Where have you been? How long were you there? What is the address of the hotel you stayed in before you entered India? Where did you stay in India? Where did you travel? Have you been to India before? Will you come again? How old are you? What is your mother's maiden name?"

On the floor of the immigration office were piles of these questionnaires, the bundles tied with rough twine, stacked in columns that reached from floor to ceiling. I was sure that in a nearby column I could see the papers I had filled out a few days before.

What became of all these tied up bundles, I wondered.

When the British passed the India Independence Act of 1947, India achieved self-government, but then came a host of serious difficulties. Fighting and massacres between Hindus, Sikhs, and Muslims eventually ended in communal segregations. Muslims fled to Pakistan; Hindus and Sikh refugees struggled to the eastern part of India. Distrust and bitterness continued to this day in parts of these areas.

One commendable lasting legacy of the British remains in modern India. The people politely queue. No one pushes. No one gets out of line. Politeness prevails.

Bangkok, Thailand

By now I had an established routine when landing in a new country. Pass through customs and immigration. Pick up my luggage. Look for the money exchange. Cash two traveler's checks, enough to pay for a taxi in local currency. Find the taxi stand. Give them the name of the hotel where Buster had stayed a year ago.

"Sorry, madam. That hotel no longer exists. It burned down last summer."

Oh! Oh! Now what should I do?

"Can you take me to a hotel for nice ladies, one that is not too expensive?"

The taxi driver turned to the cabbie behind him and they spoke in a language I did not understand. Several more cabdrivers joined into the discussion, occasionally they would glance at me, then converse together for several minutes. Finally the driver I had first spoken to walked to his taxi and opened the door for me.

"I will take you to a good hotel."

We drove through streets crowded with cars, blaring horns, jaywalking pedestrians, and numerous delivery carts. Several times I was sure we would scrape the car next to us, but thanks to my adept, nimble driver, we arrived at a small hotel unscathed.

"You go see if they have a room for you. I will wait here."

The room was acceptable. I thanked and tipped the courteous driver. My faith in Bangkok taxi drivers had been established.

My first order of business was to call the minister of mines and petroleum and arrange for a meeting as per my husband's instructions. When I arrived promptly at the scheduled appointment time of 10:00 AM, I was led to an office where two men in business suits courteously greeted me. I asked for map number 2092. One of the men opened a drawer and handed me the map. I took it, unrolled my clear plastic tracing sheet, went directly to the window that was exactly where Buster had drawn it, and began to trace the minister's map.

The two startled men looked at each other in amazed silence. Finally, one of them spoke.

"Mrs. Ivanhoe, if you want a copy of that map, we can give it to you. You don't need to trace it."

As I exited the mines building, a young man of college age approached me.

"You are American?"

"Yes."

"You tell your president he must buy our rice."

The young man must have surmised I was someone important because I was visiting a government office. Alas, young man! I have no clout.

Busy Bangkok, crowded with people all rushing somewhere, shops crammed with souvenir articles in the dozens, shop windows displaying lovely silk materials I longed to touch, signs advertising made-to-measure suits in twenty-four hours. If I had the money I would have ordered several.

A tourist trip on one of Bangkok's canals looked appealing. We passed displays of gorgeous colorful tropical flowers. We saw areas of pathetic people living in squalid slums. As we drifted along, our guide pointed out elaborate beautiful, colorful temples. They looked like the Siam of old, richly decorated with slender spires and glistening tiles.

"Here is the newest most lovely temple our princess built for us," the guide proudly told us, pointing to a dazzling, brilliant golden pagoda-like structure.

It seemed to me that Bangkok already had enough temples and their princess could have used the money to better the lives of her people.

Ahead of us I watched a woman empty her chamber pot into the river, reach down, and swish it around in the water to rinse it clean.

All along the riverside, large jars of water were standing on steps and walls.

"What are those jars for?" I asked the guide.

"That is each family's drinking water," he replied.

"But that water is not purified."

"Oh, yes. They let the water stand all day. By evening, all of the impurities have sunk to the bottom. The water is then clean and fit to drink."

"Don't drink the water," my doctors had admonished. I could understand why.

No matter where I had been during the day, I was careful to return to my hotel by dusk, usually eating dinner in the hotel. As I sat down that evening, a young man approached my table.

"Hi, I'm an American. I've been traveling alone all across Thailand for over a month and it gets lonesome not having anyone to talk to. May I join you for dinner? I'm starved for the company of an American."

"I would be pleased to have you join me. But why have you been traveling across Thailand for over a month?"

"I buy temple hair."

"Temple hair?"

"Yes. The young girls cut their lovely, healthy, shiny long hair and give it to their favorite temple as a temple offering. I go to the temples and buy that temple hair."

"What do you do with it?"

"I sell it to the wig makers in America. There is an active market for temple hair."

"There certainly are a lot of ways to make a living." I smiled.

We two had a friendly visit and a tasteful meal. When time came to pay, the young man shook his head.

"No. Let me pay. I have enjoyed your company."

In downtown Bangkok, I saw many American soldiers. Occasionally one of them would walk up to me and start to talk.

"This sure is a hell of a lonesome place to be. God! How I miss my family. Will you have dinner with me?"

When I was telling my mother in Canada about my trip, I said I had declined all the lonesome young soldiers' invitations.

"Helen, it wouldn't have hurt you to have dinner with a lonesome young soldier."

"Mother, these young soldiers were much too lonesome, far too eager. I would not have felt comfortable."

Manila, The Philippines

December 23, 1965. Oh good! Warm moist air greeted me as I walked across the tarmac and drew a deep satisfying breath. It felt good not to be cold. Now if only my aggravating tooth did not flare up, Manila should be a great place to explore. I was eager to launch out.

As soon as I registered at my hotel, I phoned Buster's geologist friend Bill Merrill. His California accent was a pleasant sound to my ears.

"Hello, Helen. I've been expecting a call from you. Welcome to Manila. Helen, I must warn you about something. Do not walk out of your hotel alone. If you want to go anywhere, you call me and I will send my driver over to take you wherever you wish to go. Remember, don't walk out of your hotel."

Why would Bill warn me not to wander about? Was my hotel in a poor area? Or was the City of Manila not a safe place? Alas! There went my idea of a perfect place to explore. Restrictions had replaced unrestricted roaming. If I couldn't wander about, I would miss the sights and sounds of Manila.

Bill continued, "I would like to pick you up tomorrow at 10:00 AM and drive you around the city to show you the sights of Manila. And you are invited to have dinner with my family and some of my special friends tomorrow evening."

The formal dinner at Bill Merrill's house was a new experience for me. Bouquets of flowers graced the center of the big table that was draped in a white linen tablecloth, lovely white china, sterling silver tableware, and three gleaming crystal glasses were at each place setting. Bill's wife was away, so his teenage daughter acted as hostess, sitting graciously at the head of the table with a small silver bell at her side. When she had a request of a servant, she delicately rang the small silver bill. The servant appeared immediately.

"Madam?"

The daughter gave the order. The servant moved quietly and respectfully along the long table in response to the girl's request. Then the servant disappeared, reappearing only when again summoned by the bell. Dishes were efficiently and silently whisked away, and new plates appeared in noiseless movements.

What a way to live!

Bill Merrill had been a gracious and concerned host.

"Tomorrow is Christmas Day. Do you have plans? If not, I'll send my driver over to your hotel, and you can spend the day with us."

Bill's parting words that evening were "Now, you be sure you call me if you have any problems. Call me from any country. Don't hesitate to ask for help, no matter where you are."

When I was a small child, I thought Christmas was the most important holiday of the year. Then when I learned that Easter was the most important Christian holiday, my young mind could not fathom how that could be. There were no presents from Santa at Easter, no decorated trees, no concerts, no carols.

Tomorrow would be Christmas in a foreign country. Would there be decorations and trees and carols? Probably not. What it would be was a day spent with relatives of Jim and Doris Vernon, those treasured friends who had volunteered to be our daughter's court-appointed legal guardians. Jim Vernon's sister Jan Hannaford and her husband lived in Manila and had invited me, a grateful guest, to share Christmas with them.

On the way to the Hannaford's, I asked the taxi driver to take me to a flower stand. A bouquet of long-stemmed colorful flowers caught my eye. When I gave them to Jan, my hostess, she smiled.

"Oh, thank you. I'll take these to the kitchen."

Why the kitchen, I wondered.

It turned out that my bouquet had bugs on the long stems.

"Helen, I started to cut off the buggy stems, then I saw more bugs on the stems and had to cut even more, so this is all that is left of your lovely bouquet."

She held up a short-stemmed cluster of what was left of my long-stemmed bouquet.

"But this is still very lovely. Thank you. Here in the tropics we are used to bugs. It's just the way things are."

After a splendid and enjoyable Christmas dinner, Jim Hannaford spoke up.

"Let's take Helen for a drive and show her some of our tropical countryside."

We drove through lush jungle, so dark, green and thick and dense that our road was an opening slashed in the exotic vegetation around us.

"Oh, damn! Look what we have in front of us," Jim Hannaford hissed in exasperation.

Ahead of us I could see a wooden traffic barrier shutting off all forward traffic. Two uniformed men stood on either side of the barrier.

"They want money and I'll be damned if I'll give them one bloody cent."

"Oh, Jim, do be careful." Jan's concerned voice made me uneasy.

Jim stopped the car. One guard walked over. Then ensued a heated conversation which I could not understand. In Tagalog, they argued for fifteen minutes until finally, much to my relief, the guards took down the barrier and allowed the car to proceed.

And no, no money had been paid to the uniformed men, but Jim Hannaford did say a string of forceful swear words as we drove away. I understood those words. They were in English. Who were those guards? What did they want? I never knew.

The next morning when I boarded Cathay Pacific Airlines for Hong Kong, my face was swollen and aching with pain. Aspirin no longer controlled my throbbing toothache.

Hong Kong

"If I can just last until I get to my sister in Vancouver, I'll have this tooth looked after," I told myself.

But when I arrived at my hotel in Hong Kong, I knew I could tolerate the intense pain no longer.

"Is there a dentist nearby who speaks English?" I asked the desk clerk.

"Yes, of course, madam."

She wrote a name and address and handed me a slip of paper.

"He's a good dentist, and his office is near to our hotel."

It was a Sunday. I walked to the address to reassure myself of the location and office hours. Nine o'clock on Monday morning I was sitting on the office steps when the dentist, somewhat surprised, walked up to open his office door.

He led me into a room and gestured for me to sit down in his dental chair. As I glanced around the small room, I could see dust along the baseboards, but as I watched him carefully scrub his hands with soap and water before he asked me my problem, I felt reassured.

I pointed to my back tooth, a molar. He tapped it with a small hammer. I jumped in pain.

"Come out! Come out," the dentist declared.

When the Novocain had taken effect, it was time to pull the tooth. The dentist pulled and pulled, and he pulled and pulled some more. Not a budge. He called a helper from a back room, and the two of them pulled. Finally, the molar came out of my jaw with a tearing, ripping sound.

I bent over, held the dentist's hand, and sobbed in relief. He looked embarrassed as he patted my hand.

"That's all right. That's all right. Nobody like a dentist."

"How much do I owe you?" I asked when I stood up a few minutes later.

The dentist took a deep breath and, in a positive voice, announced "Twenty-five dollars."

I sensed that my charge was higher than normal, but I was so relieved to be pain free that I would gladly have paid even more.

As I prepared to leave, the dentist handed me a tablet wrapped in clear plastic.

"Hurt, take. No hurt, no take."

I carried that tablet in my purse for almost a year before I felt I could safely discard it. My jaw did not bother me then and has not bothered me since. The desk clerk was right—he was a good dentist.

Pain free and energized in the warm subtropical climate, I signed up for a day-long tour of the area. On the ferry boat from Kowloon to Hong Kong Island, our guide gave us some background history.

"Hong Kong Island was liberated by the British in 1945. This island is strategically important because of trade and its excellent harbor. We have a very diverse population here, Chinese, British, Indian, and even a few Americans."

When we landed on the island, our guide pointed out the New Territories, acquired from China in 1898 on a ninety-nine-year lease.

I quickly did the math.

"What happens in 1997 when that lease expires?" I asked.

"I'm sure something will be worked out," the guide replied optimistically.

North, beyond the New Territories, was mysterious Communist China, a country where no American dared to travel because the United States did not recognize the Communist regime.

Everywhere around us was activity. Men in neat business suits hurried along the clean streets. People looked healthy, busy, and purposeful.

Our tour took us to a bay where fishermen lived on their boats, lined up side by side, so close that each boat touched another with no space between. Then we traveled to the eastern side of Hong Kong Island where huge elaborate mansions clung to the hillsides. One after another we drove past beautifully manicured grounds framing grandiose homes. What a contrast to the crowded fishermen's homes.

Back at my Kowloon hotel, the desk clerk spoke to me as I entered.
"Was the dentist I sent you to satisfactory?"
"Oh, yes!"

Early the next day, I set off to explore the crowded shop-lined streets of Victoria City. Beautiful wool materials, shimmering silks, windows displaying tempting jewelry in silver, gold, and enamels.
Tailor shops with conspicuous signs:
"English wool suits in twenty-four hours. Guaranteed fit."
"We ship to America."
This was the true meaning of "window-shopping." I had neither the money nor the suitcase space to buy anything, so I looked and looked and longed and dreamed.

Prominently displayed about the city were large billboards of a colorful crouching tiger advertising Tiger Balm. *What is Tiger Balm?* I wondered. It seems that Tiger Balm was a cure-all for whatever pain you were enduring. It was good for colds, chest pains, sore muscles, aching feet, headaches, backaches, and a wide variety of other bothersome maladies. Curious to discover more about this wonder medicine, I bought a small tin only to discover that Tiger Balm looked and smelled exactly like our mentholatum and our Vicks vapor rub.

Wandering along narrow side streets, not keeping track of time or direction, I realized dusk was gathering and I wasn't sure where I was. Walking toward me was a Chinese man in a business suit.
"Sir, can you tell me which direction to Kowloon Road?"
The man quickened his pace, stared straight ahead, and completely ignored me.
I tried to ask a second man for directions, and he also ignored me. When I said, "Kowloon Road?" to a third passerby, he too went hurriedly by me. I realized I had a problem. These men must have thought I was "soliciting," not asking for directions.

On my last day in Hong Kong, I broke a United States law. Intentionally. It was illegal for a US citizen to possess items made in Communist China, but when I stepped into a shop selling Chinese items made of cinnabar, I was captivated. Cinnabar is a reddish material that could be easily carved into dishes, vases, statutes, and jewelry. A small round four-inch bowl, the lid beautifully carved with a figure on a bridge, surrounded by trees, flowers, and a distant temple caught my eye. Throwing caution to the winds, I bought it. My plan was to leave it with my sister in Vancouver, Canada, and retrieve it at a later date. In 1972, when the United States recognized Communist China, I was able to claim my bowl and bring it home to California.

Tokyo, Japan
> December 29, 1965

"Is this your first trip to Japan?" asked the lady sitting next to me on the bus from Tokyo airport into the city.

"Yes," I replied.

"You will like Japan" the lady responded. "Japan is very efficient."

In the next few days, I was to learn that not only was Tokyo efficient, it was orderly, polite, and very clean. So tidy were the streets of Tokyo that if I saw a cigarette butt on the ground, I almost felt compelled to pick it up, it seemed so out of place. If I hesitated on a street corner, a Japanese passerby would stop and politely ask, "May I help you?" Groups of schoolchildren would giggle and shyly call out.

"Hello. What is your name?"

Their teacher stood close by, smiling as her students practiced their English.

On New Year's Day, the main shopping streets of Tokyo were so thronged with well-dressed people that it was a struggle to maneuver through the crowds. I wondered why so many people were wearing white face masks that covered their nose and mouth.

It must be because they are afraid of catching someone's cold, I thought.

Then I felt almost ashamed of my first impression when I learned that the mask was worn because the wearer was infected with a cold and didn't want to spread his cold to others.

When Buster had visited Tokyo the previous year, he had chosen to stay in a Japanese-style hotel. I chose to stay in the same hotel. It was certainly different from a conventional Western hotel. The small room was very clean and very sparsely furnished. The walls were paneled in light-colored wood and lined with cupboards. The polite Japanese innkeeper slid aside bamboo doors, pulled out mats and bedding, and arranged a bed for me on the floor.

"Please, here is some hot Japanese tea for you." He brought in a teapot and a small round, handleless cup in an Oriental design.

He showed me the hot tub and instructed me on its use.

"First, we soap our bodies, then pour water over ourselves until all the soap is rinsed off. After that we step into the hot water and enjoy a relaxing soak."

The day had been chilly, and I was looking forward to settling into the hot tub. When I put my foot into the water to test the temperature, it was hot, really hot. I hastily pulled back my foot. Each time I tried to enter the water, the extremely high temperature forced me to withdraw my foot. It was unbearably hot. Finally I gave up. No Japanese hot bath for me.

The next morning when the innkeeper politely greeted me, he said, "American people cannot tolerate the hot water the way we Japanese people can."

Had he been watching me attempting to enter the hot tub?

"Be sure to plan a day when you can take the high speed train from Tokyo to Mt. Fuji. No trains in America travel that fast." Buster had told me. At last, I could see beautiful Mt. Fuji, that classic volcanic cone.

I wasn't sure if the train ticket sellers would speak English so I asked the innkeeper to write "High speed train to Fuji" in Japanese characters. After I would arrive in Fuji, I had better be sure I could get back to Tokyo so I asked my helpful host to also write out a second set of instructions.

"Fuji to Tokyo."

When I had arrived in Tokyo several days before, the lady on the airport bus had told me, "Japan is very efficient." It certainly was. My train ticket was numbered as to where on the platform I should stand to board the train. And that is where the train stopped, exactly, precisely as my ticket was numbered, not a fraction of an inch off.

The interior of the train was immaculate; the passengers were well-mannered and neatly dressed. Suddenly, I felt awkward in my well-worn travel clothes that I had been wearing for days.

Across from me, two Japanese ladies ordered a lunch that came with a cardboard box tied with a ribbon. When they opened the box, they offered me some food before they began to eat. I declined although the various little parcels looked appetizing. When the ladies finished eating, they carefully put all the food wrappers systematically back in the box, neatly retying the ribbon so that the cardboard box looked as tidy as when it had first arrived.

Before I left Tokyo, I had to go to a theater to see Kabuki, the classical traditional popular drama of Japan. The costumes and stagings were striking and dramatic, but I did not understand the play nor had I any inkling of what it was about.

My short stay in Japan was over. Reluctantly I had to leave the Orient, but I vowed to return at some future day to this clean, efficient country.

Vancouver, British Columbia

January 2, 1966

As our plane approached Vancouver, we could see that it was snowing. The closer we came to Vancouver, the denser and thicker the falling snow became, big flakes that floated past our plane windows, blocking out all visibility.

Instead of landing, we circled the city. And we circled and circled and kept on circling. Finally the captain's voice came over the speaker.

"We cannot land in Vancouver due to the weather conditions. We will fly on to Seattle and wait for further instructions."

As soon as we landed in Seattle, a man seated next to me called over a stewardess.

"Seattle is my final destination. Can my wife and I get off here? We were to fly from Vancouver to Seattle, but this is perfect and saves us a trip. May we please get off here?"

"No, sir. I'm afraid that is impossible."

"I can take care of that. Let me speak to the captain."

The man got up and strode confidently forward.

A few minutes later, he returned, crestfallen, and subdued. He spoke to his wife.

"Sorry, dear. It is against FAA (Federal Aviation Administration) rules for our captain to allow any of us off the plane while we wait for instructions to return to Vancouver. Damn it! Now we fly back to Vancouver, then fly to Seattle where we already are. Oh, damn! This is so stupid."

For an hour, I sat quietly wondering what would happen next. With relief, I heard the captain's voice.

"We have been given permission to return to Vancouver. Please remain in your seats at all times until we have safely landed."

Snow was still falling when we began our descent. I closed my eyes and prayed. As we finally disembarked, I heard several crew members congratulating the captain.

"Well done, sir. You made a great landing."

"I thought so myself." The captain smiled.

Canadian customs. Immigration. Baggage pickup. Where was my bag? Why was it so slow? And then I saw my sister Valeria smiling and waiting for me. She had never looked prettier. I was so very glad to be with my family again.

The three of us, my sister, brother-in-law, and I walked out of Vancouver airport into a world of wet falling snow. Already over two feet of the heavy white stuff covered the ground, and more was floating down.

"Oh, let's see what this little VW can do in this crap," my brother-in-law said as we all piled into his car. The little car ploughed valiantly forward until it finally sputtered and stopped in the unplowed alley behind my sister's house.

Welcome home! To be with family again, to laugh and giggle and relax amid loving surroundings—it felt so good. My sister must be the best cook in the whole world—everything she fixed tasted delicious, from buttered toast to mashed potatoes. No more exotic foods, just good old familiar dishes with no stinging surprises.

"Helen, there is someone in Vancouver who lives here and wants to see you. It is your childhood friend Amy Anderson. She wants you to come for dinner tomorrow night. Here is her phone if you want to call her."

Pleased and excited about seeing Amy again after many years, I phoned her immediately.

"Yes, Helen. You are all invited for supper. We called it 'supper' on the farm and we call it 'supper' here. We are having stew. After traveling all over the world, I hope you aren't too stuck up to be served plain old-fashioned stew."

That sounded just like my old friend Amy.

My friendship with Amy went back many, many years.

A pioneer homestead in an isolated area of Alberta, Canada, had been my childhood home. Our neighbors were few. Roads were barely passable difficult trails. All of us pioneer families had no telephones, no electricity, no indoor plumbing. Everyone had outdoor privies, coal oil lamps and woodstoves. During those difficult Depression years, no one had any cash. We were all poor together.

"I wish I had a girl to play with," I would lament to my mother. The nearest girl close to my age lived six miles away. Then the Andersons moved in one-half mile west of our home. And they had a girl, Amy, only a few months older than I.

We became friends, then we became pals, then we became buddies for life. We played together, walked to school together, slept at each other's homes, and shared our most special secrets. We were a united front.

As we grew older, eleven and twelve years of age, I noticed the boys were paying attention to Amy. She was blonde, pretty, and her movements were provocative. At twelve years, she not only had a steady boyfriend, she had several lined up as alternates. No one paid any attention to me. I was the ugly duckling, so Amy began to instruct me on how to attract boys, but I really didn't want a boyfriend. Most of the farm boys were crude and they smelled.

Amy taught me how to shoot a .22 rifle. She taught me how to ride a horse bareback, and she taught me the hop, skip, and jump. She was about seventeen when she got married and eighteen when she decided to get a divorce. The only grounds for divorce in Alberta was adultery, so Amy dyed her blonde hair black with the idea that, as a stranger, she would have sexual relations with her own husband, then sue him for divorce. Through all her amorous exploits, we remained friends. I liked Amy. When I married and moved to California, I did not see Amy for fifteen years.

On the morning of the day we were to go to Amy's for supper, the phone rang.

"Hi. It's Amy. I've been thinking of our school days at Poplar School. Do you remember how you and I could beat everyone in the races? We were good."

Amy reminisced for several minutes about our days in Poplar School. If we misspelled a word, our teacher made us stay after school and write the word fifty times on the blackboard. Amy taught me how to hold two pieces of chalk between my fingers so I could write two words at a time.

Just after lunch, the phone rang again. "Helen, you always beat me in arithmetic, but one time I beat you. You said, 'I don't care if you beat me.' The teacher heard you and made you wrote on the blackboard ten times. Do you remember writing this? 'I will do better in arithmetic.'"

Late in the afternoon, Amy called a third time.

"Did I tell you I am currently living with Mark? And did I tell you to come at 6:00 o'clock?"

Promptly at 6:00 PM, we arrived at Amy's address, the three of us, my sister, my brother-in-law, and I. We rang the doorbell. No answer. We knocked on the door. Again no answer. My brother-in-law knocked as hard as he could but still no response.

"That's really strange," my sister remarked. We moved around to a window and peered inside. In the room we saw a couch with a blanket, half on the couch, half on the floor, as if it had been hastily flung off.

We looked at each other. All three of us had an ominous reaction. I shivered.

"Something isn't right," my sister whispered.

Silently, we drove back to my sister's house.

At nine o'clock that evening, the phone rang.

"This is Mark. This is really difficult for me, but I have to tell you. Amy is dead. She died of a heart attack this evening at 6:30 PM. She so wanted to see Helen, and now she is gone. Amy is dead. I am having a hard time believing it."

Three words: "Amy is dead." My childhood friend, my pal, was gone in an instant. Amy was only forty years old when her life abruptly ended. And with Amy went some of my childhood. Part of me died with Amy that evening in Vancouver.

Most of the snow had melted when my sister drove me to the Vancouver airport for the final leg of my journey. My next stop would be Los Angeles, California.

"United States customs and immigration this way." I followed the signs. Immigration looked at my passport.

"Quite a trip you have had, young lady."

Customs looked at my small suitcase.

"Where is the rest of your luggage?"

"This is all I have."

"You've been around the world with one small suitcase? We have people who come to Vancouver for a weekend with more luggage than this."

When my plane touched the ground at the LA airport, I was glad to be back in California.

All during my trip, people had been gracious to me, a single woman, traveling alone. Now I had a better understanding of people that were so different from me, yet somehow it seemed we were all so much the same.

Thailand Temple

Chapter 7

Helen Smart at Great Buddha
37' bronze Kamakura, Japan

Helen Smart at entrance to
local Japanese hotel

Kyoto, Japan Ryoanji
Temple and rock garden.
Zen Buddist
Founded 1473

CHAPTER

8

The Rock Rolls Back to Rome

Not long after we arrived in California, Buzz Ivanhoe, geologist and geophysicist, was asked by his friend Zvi Alexander to return to Israel to review offshore seismic information. Buzz found a "prospect" (an oil term for a possible oil field), but the prospect was under permit to another oil company. Zvi quietly waited until that company's permit expired in April 1966, and by skillful negotiations, was able to obtain an interest in the prospective area known as Siglag. Zvi immediately asked Buzz to prepare a brochure to present to foreign investors. Then the two men, Zvi Alexander and L. F. "Buzz" Ivanhoe, made trips to Athens, Rome, and London seeking investors willing to put up the money needed to drill Siglag. They found the investors, but the prospect was a disappointment.

It seemed logical that we should headquarter closer to Buster's work. Why not return to Rome? A trip to Alberta, Canada, assured me that my parents and family were well. Rod was in the army. Cheryl was doing well at California Lutheran College. She was only nineteen, still not twenty-one, the age of majority, so she again needed a court-appointed legal guardian. Once more, our loyal friends, Doris and Jim, agreed to take on that responsibility.

"Sure. We can do that. Cheryl has been no problem."

In September 1966, we bounced back to Rome, eager to continue our exploration of the Eternal City.

Back in Rome at our friendly Pensione Texas, we asked if they could recommend an agent to find us an apartment for rent within the city walls.

"Signore Zanetti is a personal friend. I'm sure he can help you."

When we walked into Snr. Zanetti's office, he greeted us with that Italian gift of warmth and sincerity—as if we were old friends.

"You are in luck, Signora and Signore Ivanhoe. I have available a lovely apartment in a most desirable area. It is near St. Peter's and directly across from Hadrian's tomb, Castel Sant'Angelo, we call it. It has been newly remodeled and renovated. The signora will especially like this—it has a splendid updated kitchen with all new appliances. The rent is $150 a month. How does that sound to you?"

When we saw the apartment, we gasped in pleased surprise. The front door opened to a wide hallway of gleaming white marble. The spacious living and dining rooms with their shiny hardwood floors and huge windows faced a massive, round high brick structure. We had an unobstructed view of Hadrian's tomb, that immense monument to a Roman emperor built about 138 AD. Between our street and the huge tomb, an inviting well-kept green park framed the towering colossus. Atop the whole, an angel reached heavenward, and beyond was the River Tiber. This was Castel Sant'Angelo. *Wow!*

Signore Zanetti continued, "There is something I must explain to you. This apartment is owned by Signora Lambrosa. Each winter she goes to New York to visit her son and returns back to her place in the spring. So you can only rent her place from October to March."

"But we wanted to rent for a year," I explained.

"No problem," Snr. Zanetti replied. "In the summer many people will be leaving hot Rome for cooler places, so there will be lots of choices for you."

Piazza Adriana Undici (eleven) presented no problems; everything worked; everything pleased us. On the bottom floor, a friendly *portiere* sat in his little cubicle, two massive doors between him and the street. His job was to screen people and protect us from intruders. His three-year-old granddaughter, Mercedes, and I became instant friends. Her youthful vocabulary was well matched to my basic Italian, so we got along very well as long as we spoke only in the present tense. Mercedes often came to visit us, traipsing up the stairs under the watchful eye of her grandfather. She pounded on our door and called out loudly.

"Americana! Sono io." (American lady, it is I.)

Before long I became known in the neighborhood and to all the shopkeepers as L'Americana.

We had been in the apartment only a month when my husband was called back to Israel. By now it was November, and it was damp and cold. I shivered inside our apartment. Radiators circulating only warmish water didn't do much to warm the big rooms. And the bed felt so cold and damp when I tried to sleep. I solved that problem by luxuriating in a tub full of hot water every night, jumping into bed toasty warm.

One Sunday morning very early, the portiere knocked on my door.

"Signora, scusa" (excuse me). How often do you bathe?"

Strange question, I thought. "Every night," I answered.

"Oh! Mamma mia!" He threw up his hands. "Mamma mia! Signora, you have used up all the water for this apartment house. The water tank on our roof is empty. Signora, we have no water. Oh! Mamma mia! A bath every night. Oh! Mamma mia!"

Electricity was so expensive in Rome that the shops and restaurants did not heat their premises, but I found a place that was warm and comfortable. A small church nearby ran a movie theater that was always full of soldiers and locals like me, people trying to keep warm. All the movies were Westerns starring a lanky young fellow called Clint Eastwood.

As I left the theater late one afternoon, a young soldier followed me, calling out suggestive sexual phrases. Ahead of me I saw a priest and rushed up to him, telling him of my discomfort.

"Oh, signora, be patient with the boy. He's just a youngster, away from home and his family for the first time in his life. Signora, be patient with the lonesome fellow. He means you no harm."

No one could say that there wasn't enough to do in Rome. With my guide book in hand, I could wander in any direction, turn a corner, and discover a small piazza, an ancient Roman ruin, another splendid church, or an amusing gurgling fountain. In Rome, the Eternal City, the center of the Christian world, art was everywhere. And I was living within easy walking distance of St. Peter's, one of the stupendous wonders of the world. I never tired of visiting the Vatican. In 1966, one could walk directly inside the building, no security search, no body searches, only the watchful eye of the unsmiling Swiss Guards. Hour after hour, I moved slowly along, my guide book identifying wonder after wonder, so many treasures, so much art, so many monuments to so many people. But always that inevitable request for money from a pleading priest.

A pretty young girl in a sleeveless dress was smiling as she eagerly bounded up the steps, but before she could enter St. Peter's, the Swiss Guards stopped her.

"You cannot enter," a guard spoke sternly.

'Why?" the baffled young lady asked.

"You cannot enter. You are not allowed to enter. We do not allow sleeveless garments inside our holy building."

"But I've come all the way from San Francisco, California, to see St. Peter's."

"You cannot enter wearing a sleeveless garment."

"But I've come so far. I have dreamed of this moment for years. I'm a good Catholic."

"You cannot enter."

The young lady began to cry.

"Oh please, please let me in."

"You cannot enter wearing a sleeveless garment."

The girl turned away sobbing.

How very stupid, I thought. One of the world's grandest buildings with one of the world's stupidest rules.

As I was standing atop the steps to the entrance to the basilica, gazing at the obelisk in the center of the huge piazza, I was remembering the story of "Water on the Ropes," a story familiar to most Romans.

When the tall obelisk was brought from Nero's former palace to the Vatican in 1586, it was a solemn occasion involving 800 men, 150 horses, and 35 cranes. The large assembled crowd was ordered on pain of death to remain silent during the raising of the obelisk. At first all went well, but the tension of the ropes produced by the enormous weight of the obelisk caused the whole mass to suddenly cease to move. A sailor, in peril for his life, yelled, "Water on the ropes." In gratitude for saving the momentous operation, Pope Sixtus V granted the sailor's family the privilege of providing the palm fronds to St. Peter's for Easter Sunday in perpetuity.

I stood in admiration of the beautiful colonnade surrounding the piazza erected by that superbly talented architect Bernini. My musings were interrupted when a well-dressed man approached me.

"Do you live here?" he asked.

Oh, an American, I thought. I could tell by his accent.

"Yes," I replied, "I live here."

"Can you tell me something? Can you tell me where I can get a good Italian meal? I mean, a real meal—spaghetti and meat balls and garlic bread. None of this foreign stuff like spaghetti a la carbonara or pasta e fagioli, whatever that stuff is. I'm longing for a real Italian meal. Does such a thing exist in Rome?"

"Gee, sir, I don't think I can help you," I replied.

Eating out in Rome was an adventure. Every restaurant or trattoria posted its menu in the window. In the days before my husband had left for Israel, we had wandered the busy narrow streets, searching for the cheapest price, the best deal. We stood in front of a small restaurant carefully scrutinizing the menu when a man walked up to us.

"Qui si mange bene," he announced. Here you can eat very well.

"Si?" we asked.

"Oh si signores. Qui si mange bene. Here you eat very well."

We walked in and sat down. A few moments later, a man walked toward us as he tied on his white apron. It was the same man who told us "Here you eat well" when we were outside reading the menu.

He handed us a menu.

"We will have the fish," we announced.

"Oh, scusa (excuse please). We are out of fish today, but the bistecca (beefsteak) is very good."

"No fish? Well, in that case, we will have the pork."

"Oh, I am so sorry. We are out of pork, but the beefsteak is very good."

"Do you have chicken?"

"No, but our bistecca is very good."

"Do you have anything besides bistecca?"

"No, signores. We have only bistecca, but it is very good."

It was 2:30 in the afternoon. We were hungry, so we ordered the beefsteak. It was the thinnest, driest, most gristly meat I had ever tasted. But it had been served to us by a very enterprising owner.

In a small quiet trattoria where I often ate, a sad-looking man sat by himself hunched over a small table. When a waiter approached from the kitchen and placed a large plate of spaghetti in front of the customer, the man picked up his fork, took one bite, made a grimace, and called to the waiter.

"This spaghetti is no good. Tell the cook to bring me a fresh plate of spaghetti."

The waiter disappeared. Moments later, a stout-looking matron with a big white apron tied around her waist emerged from the kitchen, obviously the cook. She marched purposely up to the complaining man, grabbed the fork from his hand, took a mouthful of his spaghetti, and slammed the fork against the plate.

In a loud authoritative voice, she declared, "There is nothing wrong with this spaghetti. Mange! (eat)." Without another word, she strode back into the kitchen.

The sad-looking man dutifully picked up his fork and commenced to eat. Perhaps he was a widower who missed his domineering wife?

St. Peter's at Christmastime—a daily display of pageantry performed with grace and precision like a well-rehearsed opera, never a misstep or a hesitant move. And I saw it all for free.

The radiant faces of the young nuns when the pope moved along the aisle and cries of "Papa! Papa!" as he moved nearer. It was a pleasure to watch the joyous reactions of these dedicated young women.

All the cardinals in their brilliant scarlet robes sat along one side at the front of St. Peter's. Several of the elderly cardinals had young robed boys sitting alongside them. The young lads would carefully observe the older cardinal, and if the man's eyes closed and his head began to nod forward, the young boy would gently nudge the cardinal. His eyes would fly open and up would jerk the holy man's head. But before long, the cardinal's eyes closed again, and again his head would begin to nod forward.

These sleepy old men were the ones making the rules for the church?

Whenever one of Mother's letters arrived, it was always a pleasure to read the family news from Sangudo, a small village in Alberta, Canada, that had been my childhood home.

"Your father and I hope you are not alone for Christmas. Do you remember Newcombe Bentley who used to be your 4-H club leader? He is now living in Rome working for the Food and Agricultural Organization that is part of the United Nations. Give him a call, maybe he will invite you over."

Indeed I did remember Mr. Bentley. When I was twelve years old, he and another agriculturalist from the University of Alberta were returning to Edmonton, the capital city, after a late-night farmer's meeting. Mother asked if the two men would drive me to my uncle's in the city, a two-hour drive. I sat in front between the two gentlemen. Mr. Bentley put his arm around the back of my head.

"Now go to sleep, young lady. It is late."

But I was so excited, a twelve-year-old sitting between two men, that I was unable to sleep and remained awake for the two-hour drive that ended all too soon.

Decades later, I met Mrs. Bentley and told her of my twelve-year-old's girlish infatuation.

"I was in love with your husband all one night," I told her.

"Say evening," she retorted. "It sounds better."

The Bentleys did ask me to join them and their friends for Christmas dinner. It was the beginning of a long and enduring friendship that lasted until the end of their lives.

Christmas dinner was a joyous affair with many impressive United Nations guests, much laughter and interesting tales of UN activities from all around the world. One guest said his job was finding countries willing to take in displaced persons.

"My hardest task is to place black people from Africa, but eventually I find a nation willing to accept them, but it takes time, persistence, and patience."

Yvette, a young French Canadian lady kept us all amused with tales of the problems she had with the neighbors who lived above her.

"They are noisy, raucous, and obstreperous. The uproar and racket from above can be deafening. Finally I could stand it no more. I stood back as far as I could at the edge of my balcony and tossed four raw eggs into their balcony."

We never did hear what happened next.

People were still visiting when I left early in the evening. I had to take the Metro and a taxi to return to Piazza Adriana, some distance away.

Early next morning I heard the shocking news. On the way home from dinner, late Christmas evening, one of the couples stopped to change drivers. As the man stepped out of his vehicle, he was struck by a speeding auto and died instantly.

A sad, sad ending to Christmas 1966.

The new year 1967 burst upon my street with an ear-shattering thunderous cacophony of sound. From every open window above me a mass of debris was thrown onto the street below. On New Year's Eve, the Romans have a tradition of throwing out everything old: old furniture, old wine bottles (empty, of course), old kitchen equipment, old clothing, anything and everything they no longer wanted, tossed out with loud shouts of glee. What a mess when I opened my blinds at 8:00 AM, but by ten o'clock, the dutiful street sweepers had raked up all but the smallest pieces of glass.

For anyone living in Rome, an important Italian word to learn is *sciopero*. It means "strike," a work stoppage by organized employees to enforce demands for improved wages. In Rome scioperos were so common that the telephone company had a special number to call to see which employees were on strike that day. Would it be the postal workers, the garbage collectors, or the street sweepers? Each time these government employees went on strike and their demands were eventually met, the price of any product under government control was increased to cover the extra costs of the strikers' wages. So who won?

Wherever the British have ruled in territories all around the world, the people politely queue. They politely queue in India, in Singapore, in Hong Kong. The British were never in Italy. The Italians do not queue, but they have an almost imperceptible way of gently sliding past you so that the person who was behind you a moment ago is now ahead of you. As I stood in the post office in front of the stamp window, a graceful female hand appeared in front of me.

"Oh! I did not see you. Were you ahead of me? I just want a stamp. You don't mind, do you? Grazie molto. Thank you very much."

I moved as close as I could against the wicket before someone else who did not see me wanted a stamp.

Chapter 8 Rome

Helen and friend in front of Castel San Angelo (Hadrian's tomb)

St. Peter's Square with obelisk

Panorama of Rome and St. Peter's Square

Pay toilets. Instigated by Emperor Vespasian to help pay for building the Colossium

Helen and Cousin on way to St. Peter's

CHAPTER
9

Roman Potpourri

Several geologists and their wives were living in Rome. Whenever I met with them, they were friendly but extremely careful not to discuss where they were working or for whom. I met Marina, a beautiful blonde Russian girl from Novosibirsk, Russia, married to an American geologist. When Marina and her husband were established in Rome, they sent for Marina's mother, still living in Novosibirsk to join them. The mother came, didn't feel comfortable in Rome, missed all her friends, and asked to return to Novosibirsk. Why, I thought, would anyone choose to return to such a cold northerly place? When I looked at my atlas, I was surprised to see that Novosibirsk was about 54° north latitude, almost equal to where I had grown up in Sangudo, Alberta, Canada. Home is where the heart is, that is certain.

Rome was a magnet drawing peoples from all around the world; its monuments of antiquity, the decorated churches, the lavish palaces, treasures of art and history, a center of religion, literature and folklore—it was all there.

Nursie was an adventuresome young Australian nurse working in a Rome hospital. Her goal was to go around the world, working for a few months in a city of her choice, save enough money to go on to the next country, work there, repeating the process until two years later, she would return to Australia with a wealth of experience at very little cost.

My other Australian friend was Kay. Kay was a delightful lady who fell madly in and out of love. In Kuala Lumpur, Malaysia, she met the love of her life until it all fell apart. In Rome she met the true love of her life, a doctor, but that too fell apart. Now she was in love with an attorney, her noble endearing love. Unfortunately, he was married, and divorce was not yet legal in Italy, nor did he share Kay's passion. I could foresee Kay's heart to be broken again.

Kay phoned one afternoon. "May I come by with the PA to PS?"

"Yes, but what is the PA to PS?"

"Oh, sorry. This young lady is the personal assistant to Peter Sellers."

"Why would she want to come here?"

"She is looking for possible places to be Peter Sellers' hideaway in Rome. I thought your apartment might qualify."

When Kay came by with the P.A. to P.S., I saw a slender, attractive, self-assured young lady.

"What exactly does a Personal Assistant to Peter Sellers do?" I asked.

"I am to be helpful and available to assist him in anything he wishes," she replied.

Our apartment did not qualify to be a Roman hideaway for Peter Sellers.

I met Caroline in St. Peter's.

The Italian men noticed Caroline, and she responded to their comments with sexy and provocative gestures. Caroline had been the original Playboy bunny photographer, and she certainly fit the role, strikingly beautiful and with a gorgeous well-proportioned body. In New York, she had been engaged to marry a handsome young Italian. His sudden unexpected death left her devastated until she figured out her future. She would go to Italy, meet her dead fiancé's family, and marry his older brother.

"That's how it is done in Italy," she told me.

The only flaw in her plan was the lack of enthusiasm from Mario, the older brother. He was polite, constantly searching for excuses to avoid her, but Caroline was cunningly persistent. Mario finally took her to meet his family in Southern Italy. They treated her with a politeness that she mistook for acceptance.

"I was so pleased to be part of the family," she happily told me.

"After a delicious dinner, I stopped into their pretty garden for a quiet moment. Their priest had followed me. He put his arms around me and tried to kiss me. In deference to his position, I did not slap his face. Instead I kicked him in the shins as hard as I could."

Early one afternoon, a tearful Caroline phoned me. "Mario says I should go back to America. He says there is no future for me here. But I love him. What can I do?"

Later that day there was a knock on my door. I opened it to see a sobbing Caroline, suitcase beside her and a bouquet of flowers in her arms.

"He wants me to go back to America," she sobbed. "He gave me a ticket to fly back to New York this evening. And then he sent me these gorgeous flowers. I knew he really doesn't want me to go. He sent me flowers so I would stay. I think I should stay. I gave up my apartment. Can I stay with you? You are alone and you have lots of room. You have two bedrooms. I would not be disturbing you. I can't leave him. Mario is mixed up and really wants me to stay. Can I stay here with you?"

Oh, my god! I thought. *What should I do? If I let this woman into my apartment, she will never leave.*

I planted myself squarely in the middle of the doorway, fearful that she might attempt to force her way in, determined as she was to remain in Rome.

"Caroline, you must be very careful of what you do next. You want Mario to respect you, which he obviously does because he sent you this lovely bouquet. You are correct that Mario is mixed up. He needs time to sort out his feelings and he can do that only if he is left alone. You must respect his wishes, return to America and give him the space he needs. Once you are gone, he will miss you. Then he will clearly see how important you are to him. Don't contradict his wishes. Win his respect. Go back to the airport and return to America. When he is alone, he will realize how much he misses you."

For over half an hour, we stood in the doorway as I tried to convince her how important it was for her to return to America. Gradually it sunk in that the only way to win Mario was to leave. She dried her eyes, put on fresh lipstick, and powdered her cheeks.

"Yes, I do see your point, Helen. I must go so he will miss me."

She left. I shut the door and leaned against it in intense relief. I never saw or heard from Caroline again.

"Where do you find these girls?" Mrs. Bentley asked when she heard my story of Caroline.

There were a lot of buses in Rome, but the problem was that there were also a lot of people riding those buses. Oftentimes, a bus would be so crowded that I would be squeezed between standing passengers so tightly that I could not even raise my arm. The young Italian men gloried in pushing their bodies tightly against a young female foreign tourist. My lady friends and I agreed that no man could be that excited that quickly for that long and that he must have a salami in his pocket. What to do? Nothing, when you can't change position or raise an arm to slap his face.

The Romans were a sympathetic and kind people. Many times when I was carrying a heavy bag of groceries, a person stopped to assist me up a step or to cross a busy street. Sitting on a bus late one night, I realized I had gone far past my scheduled stop. As I got up to exit, a nun took hold of my coat and pulled me back.

"Sit down," she said. "You can't get off here. This is not a safe area. Stay on the bus. Go to the end of the line, stay on the bus, then return to your regular stop. And next time pay attention and don't miss your stop."

The winter opera season had begun. I always bought the cheapest seat, high in the gallery, but I was in Rome watching an opera, thrilled to be part of that world. From Piazza Adriana to the opera house, I rode the bus. When the opera ended late at night, I hailed a taxi. The driver would stop immediately in front of the massive apartment doors, watch as I unlocked the first heavy portal, watch me step inside, and unlock the second set of doors. Not until I was safely inside the apartment building behind those two heavy sets of doors did the taxi pull away. I was a foreign lady living in Rome, but the Romans were looking out for the Americana.

February 4, 1967. I had invited Kay to join me for dinner. When she arrived her first words were "You look sad. Is something wrong? Why are you so triste (sad)?"

"Yes, I am a bit sad. Today is my fortieth birthday. My life is half over."

Kay with her usual blunt approach replied, "No, not half over. Over half over."

I sighed. "I thought maybe my husband would phone me from Israel or maybe have some flowers delivered. But Buster thinks phone calls are only for emergencies and flowers are only for funerals."

Kay hugged me. "Come on, Helen. Let's go for a walk, and I'm going to take you to my favorite trattoria for a big bowl of the best spaghetti in Rome."

When Columbus discovered America in 1492, Rome was already 2,245 years old. According to legend, Romulus and Remus, the twins suckled by a she-wolf, founded the city in 753 BC. Over the following centuries, Rome rose to become the largest most powerful empire in the world. A surprising number of the rulers of that mighty empire met violent deaths.

Julius Caesar was assassinated. Tiberius was murdered by suffocation. Caligula was assassinated. Claudius died of poison. Nero committed suicide. Domitian was assassinated. Caracalla was assassinated. In AD 476, the once glorious Roman Empire fell as a consequence of brutal invasion and domestic revolutions.

Every tourist to Rome wants to see the Roman Forum where Rome's history began. My first visit to the Forum was disappointing, broken columns, jumbles of rocks haphazardly strewn about, heaps of marble, ruins of arches all scattered about with no apparent cohesive plan. It hardly looked to me like the spot where the destinies of the world were discussed and immortalized. Then after numerous visits with my trusty guide book, the Forum had come alive for me. Now I could stand at the northern end, identify the restored Senate building, the Curia, name the various temples and arches along the sacred way, follow past the huge Basilica of Constantine the emperor who accorded Christianity equal rights with other religions, all the way to the Colosseum beyond the Forum's southern end. As I stood on a slight terrace overlooking this ancient collection of Rome's history, a well-dressed man approached me.

"Can you tell me what that building is?" he said, pointing to the Senate, the only reconstructed building in the Forum.

"Oh, yes" I replied, proud that I could show off my recently acquired knowledge.

"That building is the reconstructed Roman Senate Building. It was built by Julius Caesar and is where the Senate Council met. Julius Caesar would have been assassinated in that building, but it so happened that this building, "the Curia," was undergoing some repairs. The senators had to hold their session at the nearby Theater of Marcellus, and that is where Caesar was assassinated."

Pleased that I had an audience, I continued.

"In the Middle Ages, what is now the Roman Forum was a maze of rubbish and garbage heaps. When restoration began in the nineteenth century, that rubbish had protected the lovely original tile floor of the Senate and the outline of the ancient building remained. In 1933, the Senate building, free of rubbish, was rebuilt and restored to its original glory. You are looking at a building as it would have looked two thousand years ago." As the man turned and started to walk away, I heard him say, "I'm going to have to ask someone what the building is."

Perhaps I should simply have said, "That is the restored Curia," and not have tried to impress him with my lengthy explanation.

Our Calamity Cruise
and the Contessa

Buster was back from Israel when Signore Zanetti phoned us.

"I'm sure you remember that Signora Lambrosa will be returning to her apartment at the end of March and that you will have to vacate by then. I have in mind for you an elegant home owned by a *contessa*, but it will not be available until June. Do you want to wait or shall I find something else?"

We decided to wait for the contessa's house—we would be renting from royalty. With two months ahead of us, we decided to leisurely explore Greece and the Greek Isles. My husband looked up from a travel magazine he was studying.

"Look, Helen. Here is a cruise of the Greek Isles, Dhelus, Mikonos, Patmos, the Cyclades. This price is fantastic, only $300 for a ten-day cruise, but there is only one stateroom at this price so we had better book it immediately."

"Disappointment" is far too mild a word to describe my reaction when I saw our so-called stateroom. The front of a ship, the bow, comes to a V-shaped point. It was here, far below all the decks that I opened our door and saw two bunks riveted to the metal walls, one on either side of the *V,* each bunk about a foot above the floor. So confining was the space between these hanging bunks that we did not even have room for our suitcases. They had to be stored outside in the narrow hall. No porthole, no light, no décor, just two gray bunks and two gray walls.

That night, a wave of claustrophobic panic took hold of me. Nothing bothered my sleeping husband, but I could feel these narrow sides closing in on me, pressing against my chest as I tried to breathe. I had to get out before those walls crushed me. Gasping for breath, I rushed outside into the narrow hallway.

"Calm down, Helen. Calm down. Breathe in. Breathe out. Calm down," I kept telling myself as I leaned against the cold metal wall to bring back a feeling of reality. Finally breathing normally, I was able to fall asleep only to be awakened by a thunderous, loud, grinding clanging of metal against metal, a rasping booming sound that seemed to be right beside me. It was right beside me. We were docking and the anchor was being lowered, scraping against my side of the ship. How long was that massive anchor chain before that clanking grinding would finally cease?

Nine more nights! Nine more nights of claustrophobic confinement. Could I survive? I had no choice, I had to survive.

The rest of the ship was spotlessly clean with pleasant promenades and elegant salons. We chatted with an American couple who were delighted with their luxurious stateroom.

"Come see our place. It is spacious and lovely. We are so pleased with our accommodations."

After they gave us a tour of their cabin, they suggested, "Now maybe we can see yours?"

"This is not a convenient time," I replied.

In high school, I had asked my teacher, "Which civilization is older, the Roman or the Greek?"

"The Greek is older, Helen, much older. The earliest Greek civilization, called Minoan, goes back to 3000 BC."

We saw that ancient Minoan civilization on the Greek island of Crete. We wandered among the bewildering ruins of Knossos, the palace of King Minos and home of the maiden-eating Minotaur, all the while trying to envision grandiose rooms out of the ruins. It was on the broken grand staircase leading to the ruined walls of the throne room that I heard a teenage boy lament to his parents.

"Why do we have to come to all these busted up cities?"

"Busted up cities" were plentiful in Greece, reminders of a lost glory. A land that was once lush and treed was now dry and arid. Early in its history, trees were cut for charcoal. Goats, the "desert makers" further denuded the land, erosion resulted and washed away the fertile soil. Plato, in 300 B.C. described Greece as "like a skeleton of a body emaciated by disease, a country of skin and bones."

We signed up for a tour of this ancient land that had survived the waves of invaders over the centuries, the Slavs, the Ottomans, Turks, Normans, Venetians, and today's modern-day looters of Grecian treasures. I had seen the Elgin Marbles in the British Museum, and now I gazed at the pediment of the Parthenon on the Acropolis and saw where these graphic marbles really belonged.

Our ten-day tour of Greece was a definite upgrade from our Aegean "cruise." We slept in real beds, had space for our suitcases and our own bathroom. My husband had loosened the purse strings.

Our Western world owes much to the Greeks. It was here in Greece that the beginnings of democracy first emerged. Here too, in 776 BC, the first Olympic games originated at Olympus. The influence of Greek architecture on Western architecture is evident today in many beautiful buildings throughout America.

At Mycenae we learned of the legends of Agamemnon, of Homer's Trojan War stories, of how Helen, wife of the king of Sparta, started the war when she was abducted to Troy. We saw beautiful friezes of Amazons fighting the Greeks. In Rome's museums I would often read "third-century Roman copy of a sixth-century Greek original." Now I could visit the museums with the beautiful, elegant original sixth-century marble statues so perfect that the cold marble looked like warm flesh.

In our travels, we had learned very early on that it was wise to arrive at an airport well ahead of flight departure time. We arrived at the Athens airport en route to Rome to be greeted by a disappointing notice, "Flight delayed. Two hour delay."

I sat down to read our Arthur Frommer's book *Europe on $5 a Day* when a well-dressed couple walked by. The lady stopped and glanced at my book.

"Europe on $5 a day? I do not believe it. That is impossible."

"No," I replied. "You can do it if you are careful."

"Five dollars a day! What kind of a room can you get and still be able to eat on $5 a day?"

"Well, the rooms are spartan. The shared bath is at the end of the hall and the meals are plain."

"That may be okay for some people," the well-dressed lady answered. "But that's not why my husband and I come to Europe."

In the waiting room, there were two couples with young children. The children raced back and forth between the seats, yelling and screaming. I had to tuck my feet under the seat to avoid being trampled on as the children screeched past. Their parents were reading, never looking up, never speaking to their disruptive children, completely ignoring the antics of their offspring, acting as if they didn't know those rude youngsters existed.

A little of such antics went a long way to disturbing the peace of our waiting room. I walked into the gift shop, hoping for a bit of quiet.

The shopkeeper greeted me. "Hello, are you one of those cap-pitt-oo-lists from America?"

An American walked into the gift shop. He picked up a small Greek vase and called out to the shopkeeper in a loud voice.

"How much is this in *real* money?"

No wonder we Americans leave an unflattering image behind us.

I watched as another couple walked into the gift shop to browse. The man spoke to his wife.

"There is a small marble bust I would like to buy, but all I have is $100 traveler's checks. If I cash one of my checks, I will get a lot of change in Greek money that I won't be able to spend because we are leaving. You have $20 traveler's checks. Would you cash one of yours so that I don't end up with a lot of Greek drachmas?"

Her abrupt reply? "Cash your own, you tightwad."

Maybe I wasn't the only wife with Scrooge for a husband.

Back in Rome, we visited Signore Zanetti's office to pick up the keys to the contessa's home.

"The contessa cried when I told her I had rented her home to Americans. She had heard so many stories of how irresponsible Americans were, but I assured her I knew the Ivanhoe family and not to worry. I assured her the Ivanhoe family would respect her property."

The contessa's home, Via Archemedis 19, was some distance from the center of Rome in a pleasant district called Parioli. We were not disappointed. The home was tastefully furnished with beautiful antiques. Elaborately framed pictures graced the walls and elegant draperies covered the huge windows. On tabletops, silver bowls, silver candlesticks, jade carvings, and marble vases gave us notice of a lady of exquisite taste.

The contessa obviously had accepted Snr. Zanetti's word that the Ivanhoes were dependable renters, or so I thought.

At mealtime I looked at the impressive heavy antique dining chairs with their purple velvet seats at the huge dining table with its massive elaborate silver and crystal centerpiece and thought, *I won't feel comfortable eating here for fear of breaking something.*

"Let's just eat in the kitchen," I suggested to my husband.

Two days later a woman appeared at the door.

"I am the contessa's maid. She sent me to see how you are getting along."

When the maid saw that we were preparing to eat in the kitchen, she was aghast.

"Oh no! You must not eat in the kitchen. That is only for servants. You must eat in the dining room like ladies and gentlemen. I will serve you at each meal."

And serve us she did. For three days, the contessa's servant hovered over us. It was a relief when she finally left. Later we learned that the contessa had sent her maid to check on the Americans. No matter that Snr. Zanetti had vouched for us. She needed to see for herself via her trusted maid what kind of people Signora and Signore Ivanhoe really were.

Away from the critical eyes of the contessa's maid, we continued as before, eating at the servant's table.

The light in the kitchen was low with only a sixty-watt bulb. I suggested to Buster that he buy and install a one-hundred-watt bulb. But when he did so, we could see how discolored and marred the walls were, so we reinstalled the sixty-watt bulb.

"What you don't see, don't hurt you none." Buster laughed.

Evidently in Rome royalty lives one way and servants live another way. For six months, we lived a pleasant life—royalty in the gracious living room and a servant's life in the kitchen. When we left the contessa's home, the portiere in charge of the complex said we were the best renters he had ever met. Never once did we waken him to let us in because we had lost our keys.

Signore Zanetti had left a message for us with the contessa's portiere.
"Signora Lambrosa has again gone to New York to spend six months with her son. She was delighted with the care you took of her apartment and is anxious to rent it to you again."

CHAPTER

11

Piazza Adriana, Hello, and Goodbye

We returned to Piazza Adriana Undici to be greeted by the portiere with enthusiasm as if we were dear old friends. Mercedes, his little granddaughter hugged me.

"Buon giorno, Americana."

"Hello, American lady."

When we stepped inside Signora Lambrosa's apartment, it felt comfortable, like coming home. We knew exactly where everything was. We were back in the center of the city, back among the antiquities, back where the action was, back to our favorite spot in Rome.

One big change had taken place in our eight-month absence. The portiere was a changed man, confident, self-assured, and projecting a glow of pride. What was behind this? The portiere had a car, the very first automobile he had ever owned, a small gray Fiat 500, the Cinquecento so popular with the Romans.

"It is a splendid car," he told us. "I can park it in the smallest of places, and it uses very little gas."

Several times a day, the portiere walked over to his prized auto, dusted it, walked around it, touched it, and dusted it again.

"E enamorato." His wife smiled as she watched him. "He is in love with his car."

One Saturday afternoon, shortly after we had moved, the contessa phoned me.

"I want to thank you and your husband for taking such good care of my property. Signora, I have found something that belongs to either you or to my nieces. Can you please come alone on Sunday at two o'clock to see if it belongs to you?"

Why I wondered did she ask me to come alone? When I arrived promptly at 2:00 PM, the contessa served me coffee in her gracious living room, and we chatted for several minutes.

What did she have to show me, I kept wondering.

Finally the contessa got up, walked over to a small end table, pulled open the drawer, and held up two articles.

"Are these yours?" she asked.

In her hands, she was holding a diaphragm and a tube of vaginal jelly.

"No, contessa. They are not mine."

"Then they must belong to my nieces," the contessa sighed. "I thought I should ask you first."

My guess was that she had hoped the articles were mine so that she would not have to ask her nieces.

There were still so many famous places in Rome that we had not yet visited—museums, galleries, churches, the Palatine Hill where Mark Antony and so many wealthy Romans had lived, the mysterious catacombs where the early Christians had sought refuge from persecution—we had to establish our priorities.

So we started with the most important. We took a bus to the nearby Frascati Hills to check out the source of the delicious wine we had been enjoying for many months.

Every shop in Frascati sold a female-shaped gingerbread cookie, in sizes from a few inches to an impressive twelve inches. "Miss Frascati's" distinguishing feature was three prominent breasts.

"Due per latte i uno per vino," the shopkeeper smilingly told me. Two for milk and one for wine. We did not buy a "Miss Frascati."

We sat down in a little piazza with a commanding glorious view of the vast Roman countryside. Charming villas nearby reminded us of the past glories of Roman nobles. We ordered a half liter of the famous

Frascati wine, a half loaf of crusty bread, and a chunk of cheese. When we ran out of bread, we ordered more bread. When we ran out of cheese, we ordered more cheese. When we ran out of wine, we ordered more wine. We almost missed the last bus back to Rome in our amusing attempt to come out even.

Our sightseeing trips to picturesque villages in the vicinity of Rome often began at the Termini, the big modern railroad station at the eastern edge of Rome. The Termini had been built by Mussolini who ruled Italy from 1922 to 1943.

"Sure, he was a dictator," the Italians would say. "But he made our trains run on time."

Walking toward the Termini along the street frequented by the prostitutes became familiar to us. So much so, that we recognized many of the pretty young regulars waiting for a willing tourist or an eager young Italian soldier.

On one occasion, I noticed an older middle-aged lady, neatly but plainly dressed, standing among the provocatively clad regulars. As we passed, I gasped because she looked like and reminded me of my mother, quiet, dignified and poised.

"Oh! Surely she can't be one of them. She can't possibly be selling sex. She looks like my mother."

We walked on and stopped. I looked back to see a young soldier talking to the dignified lady. The soldier nodded, took the woman's arm, and they walked away together.

"Oh, no! She looked like my mother."

"Maybe this lady was in desperate need of money," my husband said.

"Maybe this is a one-time occurrence. And look at it this way, Helen. That young soldier could have picked any one of those scantily clad females standing in line, but he selected the dignified one, the gentle lady-like one. We'll probably never see her here again."

In all the other times we walked that street leading to the Termini, we never did see "my lady" again. Maybe it had been a one-time thing by a lady in desperate need of money.

In all the popular outdoor tourist spots in Rome, there were always gypsy children with their outstretched hands and usual pleas for money.

"Io. No mamma. No papa." I, no mother. No father.

These gypsy children all looked healthy, lively, and agile. The young girls looked especially spirited and bright in their long colorful dresses.

As one girl approached my husband with her plea and outstretched hand, he adopted her begging pose, held out his hand, and in a pleading voice sobbed.

"Io, no mamma. No papa."

The gypsy girl grinned an impish grin and dropped a coin into Buster's palm. He held it in his closed fist.

"Oh, give the girl back her money," I said.

"No. I got this fair and square," he replied as he pocketed the money.

The gypsy girl shouted something which must have been unflattering because several Italian ladies who had observed the performance called out.

"Don't you give that girl any money. She has called you bad names."

In Italy if you acted in a nice way, you were referred to as "bella figura." If you acted in a not very nice way, you were called "bruta figura."

That day my husband was "bruta figura."

There were times when those gypsy children could be extremely bold and bothersome. My husband and I were walking in an isolated area when a dozen or so boys and girls appeared out of nowhere and surrounded us. I hesitated and stopped. My husband continued on. Suddenly hands were pulling at my skirt, at my coat, at my sleeves. They were all around me, circling me like a swarm of flies, calling, "Give me money. Money. Money."

"Buster!" I cried out, but my husband either did not hear me or chose to ignore me. Furious at my husband's nonresponse to my plea for help, furious at the pestering children, I swung my heavy purse with all my strength in sweeping arcs and shouts of "Vaminos!" I do not know if I shouted in Italian or in Spanish or in a made-up word, but the hoard of gypsy children disappeared as quickly as they had come.

That day I was "bruta figura."

Christmas was approaching. Remembering how grateful I was to the Bentleys for befriending me last Christmas, I wanted to be a "bella figura" and do something nice for someone.

The big Catholic hospital near us was run by efficient and kindly nuns. When I arrived at the hospital, a few days before Christmas, I was greeted by a stern-looking, no-nonsense sister.

"I'm an American living here in Rome. Is there any English-speaking person here in the hospital who has had no visitors? I've brought a little Christmas token to give to someone who is alone if you think it is appropriate, sister."

The nun gazed at me for a few seconds.

"Yes, there is an American man who is alone, but he is married and you are too pretty to be visiting a married man whose wife is not here."

"Oh, sister, I too am married. My husband encouraged me to visit someone because he knows what it is like to be alone in a foreign country at Christmastime."

The sister relented and led me along a spotlessly clean corridor to a sunny room.

"Signore Roberto, an American lady has come with Christmas greetings. Do you wish to see her?"

Signore Roberto was an American engineer working in Tripoli, Libya, and had been hospitalized in Rome for the treatment of severe ulcers.

"My wife stayed with me for several days, but she had to return to Tripoli to take care of family affairs. I think I'll be here for a few more weeks."

"Are you getting good care?" I asked.

"Yes, but I am getting fat. It's all that milk they are giving me for my ulcers."

In the next few weeks, I dropped by the hospital several times, and Bob, as he asked to be called, seemed pleased.

"It breaks the monotony."

We agreed that when he was released from the hospital, Buster and I would invite him to dinner at our home at Piazza Adriana 11.

When Bob phoned to say he was being released and could visit us the next day before flying back to Tripoli, I invited him to dinner at 5:00 PM.

"Great! Can I bring my dog?"

I hesitated.

"He is a very well-behaved dog and will be no problem."

I hope so, I thought. When Bob arrived at our door with his big black dog, he spread an ample supply of newspapers across our white marble entry and ordered the dog to lie down. Then he undid a parcel he was carrying and put in front of the dog a big thick red piece of prime beefsteak, an expensive piece of meat that my husband and I would never have considered buying. The dog tore into the red mass with ferocious bites, burped, then quietly lay down.

Where had this dog been during the weeks Bob had been in the hospital, I wondered.

After a pleasant evening, we parted company, sure we would never see each other again. Never would we have imagined that we would meet in Tripoli, Libya, several years hence.

"Want to buy a castle? There is one north of Rome advertised for sale and we have made an appointment to see it Saturday afternoon. Want to come with us?"

The phone call was from our Canadian friends, Ted and Trudi Meek. Ted was a retired engineer who was checking out Rome as a place to retire. We had come to know them well and found them to be interesting and pleasant company.

"Sounds like fun. Count us in."

"We'll be riding with the top down, so tie your hair up securely," Trudi advised me. Ted and Trudi delighted in driving their little convertible at the fastest possible speeds on Rome's narrow streets and drove "like a bat out of hell" when they reached the countryside. In spite of Trudi's warning my hair scarf blew off within minutes, lost forever somewhere in the bushes at the side of a Roman road.

Our first glimpse of the castle was not at all impressive, more like a rambling two-story irregular stone building with no outstanding features except three chimneys rising high above the gray, colorless structure. As we walked toward the castle entrance, we were greeted by over a dozen neatly dressed men and women lining the trail, respectfully bowing to us as we passed by. They were obviously workers from the castle and grounds showing their respect to the people who might become future castle owners and their overlords.

At the castle entrance, a massive thick wooden door stood open. A few feet from the door, against the stone castle wall, was a large brick outdoor oven still warm from a recent fire. I could see a few smoking embers inside.

"I hope this isn't the castle's kitchen," I laughed. As it turned out, after a tour of the castle, we realized this oven was indeed the castle's kitchen.

The medieval structure was cold and damp; there were numerous rooms on differing levels, few windows, massive stone steps, steep stairways, narrow confining hallways, high ceilings, and very little overall appeal. Everything was gray, gray, gray.

"The ad says the bathroom plumbing has been updated, so let's go find the bathroom," Trudi said.

We found the updated bathroom—a shower in the center of the room, hanging down from the ceiling that when turned on would have sprayed water across the toilet, across the sink, and across anything else in the room.

"This stone floor has a drain in the center of the room, so this isn't so bad." Buster laughed.

We did not buy the castle.

If we had any question of who was the real head of an Italian household, our question was clearly answered one afternoon in a small trattoria near the Colosseum.

One sunny day, we had gone to the Colosseum to check out the efficient sanitary system we had read about. Vespasian, the builder of the Colosseum, had installed toilets with running water for the use of the Roman public. But during the construction of this immense edifice, Vespasian ran out of money and looked for any possible way to collect revenue. He decided to tax the use of the Colosseum toilets—the world's first "pay toilets."

His advisors asked, "Is this a decent way to raise money?"

Vespasian is reputed to have answered.

"Their money doesn't smell."

Engrossed in the fascinating sights within the Colosseum, we forgot the time until hunger made us aware that it was well past noon.

"Let's find some place nearby to eat," Buster said.

Finding a place to eat in Rome should have been simple enough; the choices were many, but not for us. We had to find a trattoria with a posted menu and prices to suit my husband's frugal pocketbook.

"This looks like a nice spot," I called out.

"No. It is too expensive. Let's go on."

It was almost two o'clock when we located a small plain little spot serving meals. The door was open, three steps down led to an unadorned windowless room, nearly empty except for a table where four men sat on benches at a wooden table, laughing and drinking wine.

"Well," Buster spoke with satisfaction. "This must be a place for a good meal because these men are obviously local workers, based on their overalls and lunch buckets. Locals always know where the best bargains are."

As we sat down to order, an imposing female figure filled the doorway above us.

"Giuseppe!" the woman called out. "Shame on you. It is two o'clock and you should be back at work. Andare! Go!"

She turned and stomped away.

Giuseppe gave a nervous laugh as he spoke to his three companions, looked at his watch in feigned surprise, quickly drank the rest of his wine, picked up his lunch bucket, and stood up to leave.

No sooner was he out of sight than the three remaining men looked at their watches, hurriedly drank their remaining wine, stood up, picked up their lunch buckets, and they also left.

Back to work at a Roman wife's orders!

A telegram arrived from Medford, Oregon, the town where my husband had spent his childhood.

"Auntie Hamlin passed away Monday." Stop. "Funeral Friday." Stop. "Can you come?" Stop.

In 1965, a telegram was the most efficient method of important communication. These were the days long before cell phones or the Internet. Telephones were expensive, and long-distance phones were unreliable, so urgent messages were sent by telegram. The sender paid for each word, carefully keeping his cable as brief as possible to lessen the total cost.

Auntie Hamlin was the only mother Buster had ever known. He was three years old when his birth mother died, leaving his widowed father with two other small children. When Mr. Ivanhoe, an engineer, received an excellent job offer in Rio de Janeiro, Brazil, he was faced with a quandary.

"How can I possibly accept this outstanding job and still care for my three youngsters?"

Everyone in Medford sympathized with the widowed father. Mr. Ivanhoe was fortunate in finding three married sisters willing to become foster mothers to each of his three children.

When Mr. Ivanhoe delivered his young son to Auntie Hamlin, the lady who had offered to care for the boy, he said, "This is my three year old son. His name is Lytton."

Auntie Hamlin looked at the slight, blonde waif and announced, "That's a terrible name for such a little child. I'm going to call him Buster."

So Buster he became.

My husband recalls his twelve years in Auntie Hamlin's care with loving kindness.

"There is no way I can go to Oregon for the funeral, but I'm going to send a bouquet of flowers by wire in Auntie Hamlin's memory."

He filled out a card.

"With love from Buster."

"It would be nice if you wrote, 'From Buster and Helen,'" I said.

"She's my mother, not yours," was his curt reply.

When Trudi Meek, our Canadian friend, phoned one Wednesday afternoon, I detected a note of concern in her voice.

"Helen, I have a favor to ask of you and Buster."

"What is it Trudi? Is something wrong?"

"No. Nothing is really wrong. It's just that Ted and I have to go to London for a week on emergency business. Our little convertible car is in a garage for repair and must be picked up Friday, but we won't be here. Can you or Buster pick up our car and drive it from the repair shop to our house?"

"Oh, Trudi. I am so sorry. Buster is in Cairo on business and I wouldn't dare to drive a car on a Roman street. The traffic is horrible."

"Helen, we have no one else to ask. If we leave the car in that garage beyond Friday, it will not be insured. And I dread leaving our cute little car uninsured over a weekend in a repair shop. Please, Helen. We'll draw you a map and write out directions on how to get from the garage to our house. Please, Helen."

I relented.

"Oh, thank you. We'll come by this evening with the keys, directions, and money for your taxis."

Very early the next morning, I took a taxi to the garage to pick up my friend's car. My thought was, the earlier I got started the less traffic I would encounter.

With great trepidation, I slowly drove Trudi's car out of the repair garage onto the street only to be greeted by several lanes of fast-moving autos whizzing by me. I said a quick prayer as I pulled into the nearest lane. With Trudi's street directions carefully memorized, I was reassured that I could safely navigate to the Meek's house. But then a series of directional signs loomed before me. Where to go? Left or right? Which lane to be in? I quickly turned on the hazard signal and sighed with relief as all the Italian drivers gave me a wide berth. I would imagine the men thinking, "Give that dumb blonde tourist lots of space."

The hazard sign on, both hands tightly clutching the wheel, my head bent forward, not daring to even look sideways, I navigated the several miles to the Meek's house with lights flashing.

What a relief to have safely deposited their little convertible in their own garage without a scrape or a scratch, and not even a Carabinieri's warning. The patron saint of inexperienced drivers had watched over me that day.

Early in March, the phone rang. It was Signore Zanetti.

"Buon giorno, Signora e Signore Ivanhoe. I am sure you are aware of this, but as Signora Lombrosa's agent, I am obliged to call you and remind you that on March 30, Signora Lombrosa will be returning to her apartment. Do you need any assistance in vacating Piazza Adriana Undici?"

Before we left Rome, we decided to pay a visit to the Monte de Piedad, the Mountain of Mercy, the official government pawnshop of Rome. Romans in need of money would pawn their precious jewelry. If an item was not redeemed within a specific time, it was auctioned off to the highest bidder. This silent auction was open to any and all. We made a bid on a three-inch-wide bracelet in 14K gold. In 1968, the price of gold was $35 an ounce, the Gold Standard. Even at that price, the bracelet seemed expensive to us, but we boldly made our offer. We won the bracelet. Today when gold is well over $1,000 an ounce, we wish we had bought dozens more bracelets.

Arrivederci, Roma. Good-bye to Rome. Buster chose to fly directly to Los Angeles, but I was eager to see as much of Europe as possible before leaving the continent. I elected to fly to Madrid, Spain, then travel by local buses across the Spanish countryside. From there I would fly from Lisbon, Portugal, to Montreal, Canada, to visit my brother's family.

All went according to plan. By April 1968, I was back in California.

Buster was so pleased with the apartment he had rented for us in Santa Monica.

"We can save a lot of money by living here," he told me.

When I saw the apartment he was so proud of, I was disgusted. It was one big room, a bachelor efficiency unit with no appeal, spartan and bland, no view and very little light.

"Buster, I can't live here," I unceremoniously blurted out.

"Well, then you find us an apartment you can live with," he angrily replied.

That was not as simple as it sounded. Apartments were scarce and restrictions were many. No children. No overnight guest for more than five days.

"You mean if my mother comes from Canada to visit us, she can stay only five days?"

"Those are the rules," the unsmiling agent replied.

During the two years we had lived in Rome, I realized we had been wrapped in a cocoon. The vociferous protests against the Vietnam War had not enveloped us. And those big signs on the rear of the city buses, "Rosemary's Baby." What was that about?

Eventually I found a pleasant two-bedroom apartment on California Street in Santa Monica. We called the storage company to deliver the furniture we had stored two years ago. We bought a car. I filled out change of address cards. We settled in.

Three months later, we again contacted the storage company, this time to put our household items back into storage.

We were going to Tripoli, Libya.

CHAPTER 12

Tripoli, Libya

When the phone rang one morning in early April 1968, another challenging adventure opened up for the Ivanhoes.

"Hello, Buster. This is John Carver calling for Occidental Petroleum. Would you be willing to go to Tripoli, Libya, as our acting chief geophysicist for a short period, say six to eight months?"

"I might," Bus cautiously replied. "What's the deal?"

"Oxy has obtained a very promising concession in Libya, and we want to start drilling as soon as possible. It is taking us longer than we expected to get a long-term working visa for our chief geophysicist, but we can get a six-month temporary visa for you if you agree to our offer."

"So, what's the offer?"

"We'll pay you an attractive salary. You and Helen will be provided with a free apartment and a car. Helen's visa can be issued for only a sixty-day period, and we will pay all her expenses to go to the Libyan consulate in Rome to get a visa renewal. Oxy will provide Helen with a maid. You will both have health coverage as soon as you sign our agreement."

"When do you want me to go?"

"Immediately."

Occidental Petroleum Corporation (Oxy) was formed in 1920, but it was not until 1957 when Armand Hammer teamed up with Gene Reid Drilling Company of Bakersfield, California, that Oxy took off. Hammer had the money. Gene Reid, an engineer, had the drilling equipment and the know-how. They made an aggressive team and immediately began building their staff with the best geologists, geophysicists, engineers, and technicians, hiring them away from existing companies. They did not offer a position to L. F. Ivanhoe. As he watched his fellow oil men join the energized Oxy team, his hurt feelings grew into a mild resentment.

But money talks! Buster accepted Oxy's offer.

As in so many oil company families, the husband went off to his new position and the wife remained behind to take care of the moving details. I called the storage company, sold the car, filled out change of address cards, stocked up on medications, and said good-bye to my family. Thirty days after my husband had left California, I was flying to Tripoli via Rome to join him.

The history of Libya is an ancient one. It was colonized by Greeks and later ruled by Romans. For almost three hundred years, this part of North Africa was a territory administered by Turkey. From 1801 to 1805, the United States was at war in Libya fighting a governor appointed by the Turkish sultan. In 1803, the US frigate, *Philadelphia*, ran aground on the shores of Tripoli, and its crew of three hundred men were captured by the Turkish governor. The captured Americans were liberated by an army of five hundred mercenaries and nine US Marines.

As a result of this battle, the US Marine Corps hymn "from the halls of Montezuma to the shores of Tripoli" boasts of the wide-ranging experiences of the Marines.

In 1911, Italy, under Mussolini, began a conquest of Libya. Not until after World War II, in 1947, did Italy renounce all claims to Libya. In 1951, Mohammed Idris was proclaimed king, issuing a formal declaration of independence. At that time, the Libyan population was poverty stricken and mostly illiterate. To help alleviate the situation, the United States stepped in with economic and technical aid. In return the United

States was allowed to maintain military bases in the country. In 1968 when we arrived in Tripoli, Idris was still king of Libya.

"Posh" our Oxy apartment wasn't. "Plain" it was—living-dining room, with two windows, small bedroom, kitchen with few cupboards or shelves, one bath, one tiny one-half bath, dark green asphalt tile floors, and white freshly painted walls, all with minimal plain but adequate furnishings. From our second-story windows we looked down onto a busy street and across at a blank concrete wall that was the back of the prince's palace. If I craned my neck sideways, I could glimpse a peek of the Mediterranean Sea at the end of the street below us.

Good! We had a telephone, but as I was to learn later, it was often out of order. When it did work, it was a test of one's perseverance to dial and patiently redial until a call finally went through. Too many people. Not enough phone lines.

The day after my arrival in Tripoli, Oxy's manager of domestic help" phoned me.

"Your maid is called Zayna. She will arrive tomorrow at nine o'clock and will come one time a week every Monday for two hours."

What could I have a maid do in this tiny apartment?

Promptly at 9:00 AM, a figure draped in a black sheet arrived at our door. A finger held the dark shroud around her face so that only one eye was visible.

As soon as she stepped inside, she flung the garment off with a flourish.

"Me Zayna. Missus, you no put on floor. This put on wall."

She pointed to a small cotton mat with Arabic letters that my husband had purchased in the Suk (local market) and I had placed in front of the door.

Zayna and I never established a good relationship. Nine o'clock was her scheduled arrival time. Ten o'clock was usually her actual arrival time.

"Zayna, why are you late?"

"Missus, me slip on a banana peel." She laughed as if to say, "Are you naïve enough to believe me?"

Another time her excuse for arriving late was "Missus, me sleep late."

One Monday morning the excuse was "Missus, me get lost."

When the apartment had been painted, white globs of paint had been spilled on the green asphalt tile floor. I gave Zayna a foam pad to kneel on and a knife to scrape off the paint drops. After about five minutes, Zayna stood up.

"Missus, this Ramadan. This too hard for me."

She sat down, looked at her watch, then gathered up her black chador and left.

Why was I putting up with a maid who was an inconvenience? Each Monday I had to set aside something for her to do in this small apartment. It was simpler to do the chore myself rather than wait for her arrival.

I didn't need Zayna. I did not want Zayna. I decided to phone the manager of domestic help and tell him so.

Pulling up a chair next to the phone, I dialed his number. Busy. I dialed again. Busy. The telephone was an old-fashioned rotary dial phone. I tried again. Busy. After fifteen tries, the call finally went through.

"I do not care to have Zayna come around anymore. She is not dependable."

"Oh, madam. You must keep her. She needs this job."

"If she needs the job, she should arrive on time. I do not want a maid."

He implored me to keep Zayna. I refused. Reluctantly he agreed.

"Very well, madam. We must find another job for Zayna."

The office where my husband worked was a short distance from our apartment, so Bus chose to walk home every day for lunch.

"You had better get a supply of food on hand because I would like to bring some of the Oxy guys back here for lunch. There is a supermarket four blocks away so you should check it out to see what is available in Tripoli."

Early the next morning, shopping bag in hand, I set out in the direction of the supermarket. When I stepped into the first side street, there was no question of where I was. I was on the street of butcher shops. In front of each shop, a large metal hook protruded out from the wall, and there in the open air, hanging over the sidewalk was a complete beef carcass, slit down the front, guts out, the thick beefy hind quarters swinging below, almost touching the sidewalk. Black-robed women walked nonchalantly by. For them this was just an ordinary display of fresh beef.

I went inside.

"Do you speak English?"

"A little."

"I would like two kilos of beef please."

The owner walked outside, hefted the carcass off the hook, threw it across his wide counter, took a broad heavy hatchet, swung it down hard, and hacked off a portion of the right front leg. When he weighed it, it was almost an exact two kilos of meat and bone.

To our surprise, the beef was flavorful and tender. Later I learned that it came from Yugoslavia.

From the street of butchers, I wandered to the right, following my nose to the tantalizing smell of fresh bread. The bakery was behind a blank wall, but out in front on the bare dirt street was a crude wooden table stacked with long thin loaves of warm freshly baked bread. Two elderly Libyan men sat on a bench, leaning against the bakery wall. They looked at me and laughed, pointing to my bare arms. I was to them, an infidel, not a proper chador-covered female.

The bread smelled so good that I bought several loaves. When I broke off a chunk, it was the most delicious flavorful bread I had ever tasted, crusty and good.

A young man emerged from the bakery, his arms loaded with loaves. He stacked them into the basket of his bicycle and pedaled off. When I got to the supermarket, there was the same young man, kneeling on the floor, stuffing each slender loaf into a plastic bag, carefully tying it and placing it on the supermarket shelf. The American women had wanted their bread in plastic wrappers so the shopkeeper had obliged.

"If the American women want their bread in plastic wrappers, I'll give them bread in plastic wrappers," the owner declared.

The Oxy expatriots (the expats), American, Canadian, and British, were all very friendly to us, and we soon had a small circle of compatible friends. We expats made our own entertainment with get-togethers, parties, and dinners at each other's homes, mixing very little with the local populace. We all kept a low profile.

But one young American wife shocked us expats by having a brief affair with a handsome Libyan man. Another American wife amused all of us when she became suddenly ill with an undefinable illness the moment her plane touched down on Libyan soil, but her mysterious malady disappeared immediately when she rented a posh apartment in London. She hated Libya. She flourished in London. Of all the expats, one of the most popular was a young engineer who designed a contraption with yards of copper tubing that produced "white lightning," moonshine, for our parties. It was our only source of alcohol in Tripoli.

Most of the expats lived in an area called Georginpopoli. The streets had no names. The houses had no numbers.

How does one get to a house with no street names and no house numbers? Typical directions from a dinner host would be "Turn onto the main street through Georginpopoli. Drive three blocks. Turn right. Continue driving until you come to The Yellow Chicken Café. Our house is the fourth one past the Yellow Chicken, on the right side of the street."

All of the houses rented by the expats were pleasant and individualistic, but they often bordered on a vacant lot of weeds, litter, and miscellaneous debris. There was no zoning in Tripoli, nor were there any building restrictions.

My husband came home from the office one noon with a message.

"That man Bob that you visited in the hospital in Rome learned that we are living in Tripoli and he has asked us for dinner next Sunday night. What shall I tell him?"

"Tell him yes, and be sure to get directions."

Few houses had telephones, so messages were always sent husband to husband at the Oxy office, then delivered to the wives.

Early Sunday evening, we set out for Bob's house. We enjoyed having our own car and were glad that we were not dependent on unpredictable Libyan taxis.

"Read me the directions," Buster said.

It says, "Drive four blocks on the Georginpopli Street, then turn left. Continue to Betty's Beauty Shop, then turn right three blocks. We are the second house on the right."

We drove four blocks and turned left, looking for Betty's Beauty Shop, but we did not see it.

"Are you sure you read the directions correctly? Read them again," my irritated husband said.

We turned around and tried again. "Maybe we didn't go far enough. Maybe Betty's Beauty Shop is farther on? We drove up and down several streets with no success. No telephones. No one to ask. Buster was becoming more and more irritated.

"Let's go to that police station we passed," I suggested. "The police must have a record of where people live."

When we drove up to the front of the station, Buster angrily said, "You go inside and ask. He's your friend, not mine. I'll wait here."

I stepped into the police station and explained our dilemma to the officer behind the desk. He listened intently.

"Come with me," he motioned as he led me down a long corridor.

He opened the door to an office.

"Come inside."

Then he shut the door behind me. He stood close to me and put his hand on my shoulder.

"You got man?"

His hand moved lower.

"Him work in town?"

Then his hand rapidly slid to my buttocks.

"Or maybe him work in desert?"

"My husband is waiting for me in the car. I have to go," I hastily responded. "I have to go."

I jerked open the office door and walked rapidly back down the long corridor to the safety of my waiting husband. We drove home and opened a can of beans for Sunday supper. When I told my story to one of the Oxy wives, she said "Did you slap that policeman's face?"

"No," I replied. "Someday I might need that policeman."

Not long afterward, I met Bob at one of the Oxy parties.

"My wife fixed a really nice supper for you last Sunday and she was kind of indignant that you guys were no-shows."

"We couldn't find Betty's Beauty Shop. We tried all the nearby streets with no luck."

A startled look came over Bob's face. "Oh, my gosh. I forgot. It's not Betty's Beauty Shop any longer. It is now the Purple Onion Café. I gave you the wrong directions. Oh, please, please don't tell my wife. She'll kill me."

Just then Bob's wife joined us.

"So you are the lady who forgot about my dinner invitation?"

It was very difficult for me not to blurt out, "No lady. I did not forget. Your husband forgot to give us proper directions."

But I said nothing. Bob's face relaxed in a look of intense relief.

The ruins of two magnificent cities, impressive reminders of the ancient Roman Empire, still stand near Tripoli: Sabratha to the west and Leptis Magna to the east. Of the two, the ruins of Leptis Magna are the most extensive and interesting. As my husband and I sat eating our lunch on the curving marble steps of the huge auditorium, the white Corinthian columns behind us stood in sharp contrast to the blue Mediterranean Sea a few yards beyond. Everywhere among the vast ruins of Leptis Magna were arches, basilicas, and forums named after Septimius Severus, the Libyan born in Leptis Magna who had become an emperor of Rome. He is best remembered as the father of Caracalla, one of the most cruel and ruthless of Roman emperors, who was murdered by one of his own officers.

The ruins of Leptis Magna were a popular destination for visitors and locals alike. To protect the ancient treasures—ornamental friezes, marble statues, fallen capitols, and architectural fragments, guards patrolled these revered treasures. When I bent down to tie my shoe, a guard appeared out of nowhere.

"Did you pick up something? You are not allowed to remove anything from Leptis Magna."

Early one Sunday morning, Buster and I drove to the Jebel, the plateau five hundred to one thousand feet above the Mediterranean. Along the Libyan shore, we saw small cabins built during Mussolini's occupation. All were empty shells. These cabins had no doors, no doorframes, no windows, no window frames. Every piece of wood had been stripped from the cabins, pathetic reminders of an earlier invader.

Our drive into the empty desert was devoid of people and villages. Not until we spotted a Roman mile marker did it remind us that people had once lived here. I remembered that this coastal part of North Africa had been referred to as the Breadbasket of Rome when it was under Rome's control. Today it was a bleak, dry desert.

Libyan drivers were terrible! Cars were new to them. Roads had no rules. If you were driving south and no cars were in the northbound lane, why not drive in that lane? Two cars would race down the road, side by side, oblivious to potential danger.

Dusk was approaching when we turned around to drive back to our apartment. Ahead of us, I could see an automobile being driven erratically from side to side.

"What's that car ahead of us?" I asked.

"It's a VW, a Volkswagen."

"What's that in the backseat? It looks like sheep."

As we drew closer, we could see that there were indeed sheep in the backseat of the VW. Two big fat unshorn sheep filled up all the space in the rear of the little car. In the front seats, two white-garbed Arab men were engrossed in conversation, laughing and gesturing like kings of the road.

One weekend we attended a Libyan agricultural fair where countries from around the Mediterranean displayed their agricultural products. My only recollection is the display from Syria. Over their booth a big sign read, Our Date Have No Cholera. We never ate another date during our stay in Libya.

Buster enjoyed bringing coworkers from the office home for lunch, so it became my responsibility to have a supply of quick meals on hand. When I bought canned food at our supermarket, I was often disappointed upon opening to find that the food was stale. I quickly learned that "shelf life" in our supermarket was not the date on the can. In our supermarket, shelf life meant "until sold."

Our apartment had a tiny, uninviting guest bath, only a toilet and a sink, no shelves, no cabinets, no towel bars. I found a wooden box, covered it with a colorful towel from the Suk (local market) and made a table. I phoned the manager of domestic help and told him we needed a towel bar.

"Yes, Mrs. Ivanhoe. I will send my two best men over tomorrow to install your towel bar."

The two men arrived with a thin metal towel bar, a drill, and a screwdriver. They walked confidently into the bathroom and drilled a hole in the wall. Pleased with themselves, they looked at the wall and poised the drill ready to make the second hole.

"Don't you think you should measure where to put the second hole?" I asked.

The two men looked at each other, at me, and shook their heads.

"No, that is not necessary."

They drilled the second hole, held up the towel bar, and were surprised that the space between the holes was too wide for the towel bar. They stood back, looked again, and drilled a third hole. It too was the incorrect distance. Without hesitation they drilled a fourth hole.

"Oh! Oh! It's too low." They shook their heads in disbelief.

"Stop!" I called out. "I'm going to help you measure for this hole. We will take this tape and measure the towel bar for distance needed between the two holes. Then we are going to measure the distance up from the floor to be sure it is the same height as the first hole you drilled."

Without hesitation I began the measurements and made a pencil mark.

"Drill here please."

The two men did not move. They looked at each other.

"Here!" I pointed.

They drilled the hole. It fit the towel bar. When they screwed the bar into the wall, I complimented them.

"Thank you, gentlemen. You have done a good job."

Now we had a towel bar and three superfluous small holes in the wall. Oh, well. Maybe the men were tired. It was still Ramadan.

Libya is a Muslim country. Every year Muslims celebrate the holy month of Ramadan. It is a time for deep prayer and introspection. During the holy month, Muslims do not eat or drink from sunup to sundown. Their holy month is based on the lunar calendar and is eleven days earlier each year. When we arrived in Libya in 1968, it was during the holy month of Ramadan.

Devout Muslims pray five times a day. They stop whatever they are doing, turn to face Mecca, the birthplace of Muhammad, kneel, and pray. Their devotion is true dedication.

Every day from our apartment, we could hear the muezzin's call to prayer from a nearby minaret. Five times a day, the crier's musical loud voice filled our living room as he alerted the devout to pray.

The street below us that separated us from the prince's palace was a busy street. Frequent funeral processions passed by, always in the same direction, always a coffin surrounded by a crowd of men, all of them pushing their way close to find a space to help carry the coffin. We never saw any women in the procession.

Local buses traveled up and down that street. One afternoon, a local bus heading toward the ocean lost its brakes. The agile driver jumped out to safety as the bus and all his passengers rolled down the hill, plunging into the Mediterranean. Everyone got wet, but no one was hurt.

Buster brought home a message from the Oxy personnel manager.

"Helen has been in Libya almost sixty days. She needs to go to the Libyan consulate in Rome to have her visa renewed for another sixty days. We have made all the arrangements for her to fly there on Monday. Our driver will pick her up at 7:00 AM and take her to the airport. Our company representative will meet her in Rome. She must be sure to take her passport and yellow immunization card."

He concluded with, "She should have no problems."

I had no problems. On Tuesday, I was back in Tripoli with a renewed sixty-day visa that said, "Not valid for employment in Libya."

For the second time in recent years, I was spending Christmas in a foreign country, Manila in 1965, Libya in 1968. Buster and I decided to host a Christmas dinner with a standing rib roast. We knew where to buy the fresh beef, that "open-air" butcher shop down a side street.

"Did you know that the butchers sell all cuts of meat for one standard price per kilo?" an Oxy wife told me.

"So order the best cut and pay the same price as you would for stew meat."

The butchers were no dummies. They soon caught on that the American wives were only buying cuts of beef tenderloin and T-bone steaks. The price of prime cuts of beef went up immediately.

Buster and I sent a message to a young British couple, newlyweds Brian and Lis Barrick.

"Would you like to spend Christmas dinner with the Ivanhoes?"

"We'd love to. May we bring bread sauce and a trifle?"

The Peace Corps was well represented in Libya. We decided it would be a kind gesture to also invite these dedicated men to join us for Christmas dinner. At the Peace Corps office, I delivered our invitation to the coordinator.

"My husband and I would like to invite any Peace Corps men who are in Tripoli to a Christmas dinner at our apartment."

"Oh, no. Our young men do not need any Christmas invitations. They are all very self-reliant and are very capable of entertaining themselves. No. All our men are doing just fine."

Why, you stupid old jerk, I thought. I knew how lonesome Christmas could be so far from home. Evidently, he did not.

"May I pin my invitation up on your bulletin board just in case some young man would like to join us?"

"As you wish, but don't be disappointed if no one shows up."

Three lonesome young men eagerly showed up on Christmas day, hungry for conversation and a home-cooked meal.

Cooking in our apartment was a challenge. During the morning, the gas pressure was stable, but as soon as the evening approached, the time when everyone else would be cooking, the gas pressure was weak and unpredictable. On Christmas Day, I timed the roast beef for a six o'clock meal. It was seven o'clock when seven hungry people finally decided it was time to eat. Fortunately all our guests said they liked rare beef because rare beef is what they got.

Brian Barrick had treated his bride to a horse-drawn carriage ride to our apartment. Brian had his arms full of gifts, bread sauce, and trifle, and Lis sat in the carriage holding a huge colorful flower bouquet for their hostess (me). All went well until it began to rain. No cover over the carriage. No umbrella for the young couple.

"Brian! Look! This red paper around our bouquet is dripping all over my white dress. My dress is turning red and my flowers are wilting. Brian! What can I do?"

When the newlyweds arrived, they were laughing. Their clothes were soggy, the bouquet was limp, but the bread sauce and trifle were safe.

I opened the door to see three neatly dressed smiling young men.

"We are so pleased to be here." One young fellow grinned.

"My mother in California will be relieved to hear we had a real American meal on Christmas Day."

All went well. "This beef is perfect," Brian said. All the guests agreed.

"What I miss most here in Libya is not being able to talk to girls," one of the young Peace Corps men lamented. "We have no social life here. It's a lonesome time for us."

"Look at it this way, fellows," my husband smiled. "You are better off lonesome in Libya than you would be being shot at in Vietnam."

The United States maintained an air base in Libya, Wheelus Air Force Base, not far from Tripoli. When I learned that adult education classes were offered at the base, I decided to sign up for a Spanish class to fill my empty afternoons. Wandering about on the city's streets was not a comfortable pastime for me, the black-robed women glared at me with their one visible eye, and the men often pointed and laughed. I felt safer staying at home.

"You can't live in a cocoon," my husband declared. "You should get out and do things."

So, two times a week, at 6:30 in the evening, my international driving permit in hand, I backed the car out of our garage, said a short prayer, and set out for Wheelus Air Base. At 9:00 PM when the two-hour class was over, I drove back home. The patron saint of travelers had watched over me very well because I never had a problem or a mishap. (But I prayed a lot.)

During the months we had lived in Libya, my husband and I sensed a feeling of unease in the city. It was not something we could define, nor could we see any visible acts of oppression, but a sixth sense warned us that all was not well.

Buster had lived and worked much of his life in South America and was very aware of uprising and revolutions.

"Helen, there is something going on, but I do not know what it is. It's a feeling I had once before in Venezuela just before there was a major disruption."

"We need to make a plan to protect ourselves in case of violent demonstrations of unrest."

So together we formulated a plan. Each of us had our own emergency bag with all our official papers, some cash in small American bills and, our medications hidden in a suitcase under our bed.

"If something does happen, grab your bag and make your way to the airport," Buster advised me. "Don't wait for me. I may be unable to reach our apartment if a mob surrounds the Oxy building. Take the first plane to Rome. Go to the Pensione Texas and wait there for me. In times of unrest, the persons who get out first are the ones who survive."

We were certainly correct about our feelings of unrest. A major revolution erupted in Libya just a few weeks after we left.

When I met Jim Blom and Olly, his vivacious, petite Austrian wife, I immediately liked them both. Olly mentioned that she had always wanted to visit Egypt. What better time to go than now since we were living right next door to that ancient country?

I agreed.

"Ever since my brief visit to Cairo a few years ago, I have longed to go back to Egypt."

"Would our husbands agree that we two ladies could go off on our own for two weeks in Egypt?" Olly wondered.

Our husbands agreed, and as soon as Oxy's travel department made our reservations, Olly Blom and I were flying to Cairo, Egypt.

"Oh! Look! Look!" we both exclaimed as we flew in above the pyramids. These were words we used many times as we viewed wonder after wonder during the next two weeks.

We hired a guide, an elderly gentleman wearing a striped gray-and-white galabia, a floor-length robe. His gentle manner, his patient explanations kept Olly and me engrossed. All day long he kindly answered our naïve questions.

"Ladies, it is five o'clock, and usually my day ends now," he announced.

"Oh no. We want to see more. Show us more."

By 6:30 our guide sighed.

"Ladies. I am an old man. I am tired. But I will guide you around tomorrow if you wish."

"Oh, yes. Please come to our hotel tomorrow at 9:00 AM."

At the hotel, the personnel were extremely attentive and courteous, smiling and bowing as if we were royalty. Then Olly and I realized why we were being given "the royal treatment." The hotel was almost empty.

We were there in 1969, only a short time after the 1967 war with Israel. We represented business that the hotel desperately needed.

"Will you take me to America?" the young boy operating the hotel elevator asked us each time we stepped inside to go up to our room.

"Will you marry me and take me to America?" one of our waiters whispered.

"In America all the people are rich. Will you take me to America? Please take me with you to America."

There was an intensity and a pleading in his voice.

Early next morning when we came downstairs, our gentleman guide was waiting for us in the lobby.

"Ladies, today I am going to show you some of my country's greatest treasures across the river in the Valley of the Kings where almost all of the New Kingdom Pharaohs are buried."

"Why did they stop building pyramids and start burying the Pharaohs in this Valley?" Olly asked when we arrived at the Valley of the Kings.

"We don't really know," our guide smiled. "But some Egyptians think it is because that huge rock outcrop behind this Valley resembles a giant pyramid."

We looked where he was pointing, and yes, the outcrop did resemble a pyramid.

At first sight, the Valley of the Kings looked bleak and dry, but once we entered the concealed tombs of the Pharaohs, we were in a valley of wonders. Olly and I marveled at the extensive tombs dug into the solid rock. The vivid colors on the walls and the ceilings and the graphic painted scenes spoke of the skill of the ancient artisans. The lengthy inscriptions of the hieroglyphic writing carved into the tomb walls still stood sharp and crisp after thousands of years. Both of us ladies stood in speechless wonder at the sight of King Tutankhamen's golden glories. Such an overwhelming amount of wondrous artifacts in this dry valley!

At the end of a wonder-filled day, we thanked our patient guide.

"When you return to America, please send me copies of all the photos you have taken. Here is my name and address."

When I finally returned to California, I did send our guide copies of the photos we had taken. But I was careful not to include my return address as a precaution against it falling into the hands of one of those elevator boys or waiters so eager to come to America.

In the Cairo railroad station, I stood in line to buy our tickets to Aswan with stops at Karnak and Luxor.

"Be sure to buy first class tickets," our guide had advised. "You will be much happier."

When I reached the ticket window, the young man behind the glass nodded to my request, reached for some papers, then abruptly turned and walked away.

I waited, thinking he had gone for some documents. I waited and waited. The big clock on the wall told me the ticket seller had been away ten minutes. I spotted a janitor with a broom walking behind me.

"Do you know where the ticket seller has gone?" I asked.

"He has gone to pray. He will be back."

After an absence of twenty minutes, the ticket seller returned without an apology or an excuse and completed our ticket purchase.

Another day of wonders; Karnak with its 134 columns in a temple that is the world's largest columnar structure, Luxor and Thebes boasting a grand avenue of sphinxes that once reached all the way back to Karnak.

"We are here in the busiest tourist center in all of Southern Egypt," a local guide announced pointing to the Avenue of the Sphinxes.

"But sadly, today is not one of our busiest days."

He was correct. There were very few tourists wandering along that impressive avenue.

We were standing amid wonders from 1390 BC. We knew that the pyramids that dominated the Giza plateau near Cairo were built from 2600 BC. And we knew that the Pharaoh Menes had united Egypt in 3210 BC. But how does one gauge five thousand years of history, over ten times the history of our America? How does one put five thousand years into a meaningful perspective of time?

At Aswan, we boarded a gleaming white ferry boat to take us to Abu Simbal, site of two temples built by the Pharaoh Ramses II. We were eager to see how UNESCO was able to cut apart a mountain and reassemble those temples on higher ground before the rising waters of Lake Nasser flooded Ramses's gigantic memorials.

I settled into a comfortable chair on the deck enjoying the scenery on the way to the Sudanese border. Some distance from our ferry, I spotted a vessel traveling in our direction. It was another ferry boat, but unlike ours, this one was rusty-looking, dirty, grimy, and loaded with passengers crowding the decks.

"Thank goodness we don't have to travel on that filthy-looking vessel," I said to Olly with a feeling of smugness.

All at once, our ferry stopped. The engine had died. We were motionless in the middle of Lake Nasser.

"What is it? What has happened?" I asked a deckhand.

"We are out of oil. We cannot move until our engines get some oil."

There were shouts from our vessel to the rusty one and calls back and forth in Arabic.

The rusty vessel pulled up alongside of our clean ferry. Their captain handed our captain a large grimy can overflowing with oil. Before long our pristine ferry was moving again, thanks to the dirty, overcrowded, rusting ferry that had rescued us from our predicament.

We ladies gazed at the magnificent temple of Ramses II with the four seated colossi carved into the sandstone mountain. Nearby stood a smaller temple dedicated to the pharaoh's beloved queen Nefertari.

"Look," Olly pointed out. "Here is a powerful ruler who has immortalized the status of his glorious queen for all the world to see."

I agreed. "It looks to me as if women had more status three thousand years ago than they do today."

The two temples looked settled and secure two hundred feet above Lake Nasser—as if they had always stood there for 3,200 years. It was only when a guide led us behind the monuments that we realized the two temples were like the facings of an empty shell. UNESCO had carried out a remarkable feat of relocating those colossi from the rising waters of flooding Lake Nasser.

Our precious two weeks were almost over. When Olly and I boarded our train to return to Cairo, we talked of how much we had seen, yet as we gazed out the train windows, we realized how much more there was to see in this ancient land.

We departed Egypt with a good feeling. We were two attractive American women traveling alone who had been well received and politely treated everywhere we went—with one exception.

As we were departing our hotel for the airport, a very young boy, perhaps five or six years approached me. His short legs apart, he planted himself firmly in front of me.

"You America. You bad. Omar Sharif bad. You no good. Omar Sharif no good. You bad, bad, bad."

Whatever prompted such a comparison I never knew.

Not long after I returned from Egypt, a message came from Occidental's personnel department.

"It's time for Helen to once again visit the Libyan Embassy in Rome for another sixty-day extension of her visa."

Between Italy and Libya lies Malta, a tiny island impacted by almost every historical power in the Mediterranean, everyone from the early Phoenicians to Great Britain centuries later. On the return flight from Rome to Tripoli, the plane stopped in Malta at the capital city of Valleta. I decided to spend two days exploring this historic strategically located spot while I had the opportunity. I might never be back in the area again.

At the Valleta airport, a tiny lady seated at a Traveler's Aid desk directed me to a suitable hotel. The Maltese all spoke fluent English, so I had no problem speaking to a waiting taxi driver.

"Do you have a meter?"

"Of course, madam."

When he delivered me to my hotel, I checked the meter, which registered Maltese money.

"Can you make change for American money?"

"Of course, madam."

I handed the driver a $20 bill, and he gave me a handful of Maltese money. I had checked the exchange rate in the airport but did not carefully count the change the driver gave me.

"My name is Tony. Here is my card. If you want to go sightseeing tomorrow, please call me."

When I got to my room, I counted my change. With paper and pencil, I did some calculations. I had given Tony a $20 bill. The meter read the equivalent of six American dollars. I should have had fourteen dollars in change, but I had only $8. The driver had shortchanged me $6.

Early next morning, I walked directly to the Tourist Bureau.

"The taxi driver I had last night shortchanged me."

"We have no control over that, madam. The taxi drivers do this all the time to the tourists. You have to go to the police station with your complaint."

At the police station, I repeated my story to the officer at the desk.

"Let me see your card," he said. He dialed Tony's number.

"Tony, I'm calling from the police station. I have an American lady here who says you shortchanged her six dollars last night."

There was a short pause.

"So you do remember the lady and you will return her the money? Tony, she will expect you at the hotel at six o'clock tonight."

The officer put down the phone.

"Thank you for reporting this, madam. Tony and I already know each other. He will return your $6 for certain."

Promptly at 6:00 PM, Tony showed up at my hotel.

"Madam, as soon as I drove away last night, I said to myself, I owe that lady some more change, and I was fixing to return it to you."

I very carefully counted the bills he gave me. Not at all embarrassed, Tony smiled.

"Now that we are friends, would you like me to take you sightseeing tomorrow?"

Sightseeing the next morning would be on my own. Numerous buses and trolleys were evident in Valleta, so I hopped aboard one to go wherever it would take me. The bus tickets were purchased on an honor system, but at the first stop, an inspector climbed aboard.

"Please show me your tickets. Anyone who does not have a ticket pays double."

To my surprise and amusement, a few stops later, a second inspector came aboard.

"Show me your tickets again. I am here to check on the first inspector to see if he has correctly checked everyone's ticket."

When the trolley passed a large church, I disembarked to inspect it. A robed cleric was dusting the altar.

"Come in please, madam. Welcome. We like to have visitors."

He was friendly and began to explain the church paintings to me.

"Of course, you know that Christianity goes back many centuries in Malta. St. Paul visited Malta and Gozo in his travels as he spread the Gospel of Jesus Christ."

He continued, "I have worked in this church for ten years, working for the Lord."

"Is Malta your home?" I asked.

"Oh, no. I am not from Malta. I am from Gozo."

By the tone of his voice, I surmised that it was far superior to have been born in Gozo rather than Malta, even if the two tiny islands were only a few miles apart.

I made one last trip to the Libyan consulate in Rome. On June 2, 1969, I was issued my final visa from the Embassy of the Kingdom of Libya. In English script it read, "Not permitted to undertake any employment with pay or without."

At the end of June 1969, after eight months in Libya, Bus Ivanhoe's employ with Oxy was over. Now they had finally completed all the necessary paperwork for their own chief geophysicist to work in Libya. We were free to depart. I was ready to leave this country of anonymous black-robed women and gawking men.

We were living in Rome when we heard the news that King Idris of Libya had been overthrown. In a bloodless coup, on September 1, 1969, Muammar Gaddhafi assumed absolute control of Libya. Our sixth sense of impending trouble had proven to be correct.

Little did that poverty-stricken, illiterate population of Libya know how much their indigent lives would change and not for the better.

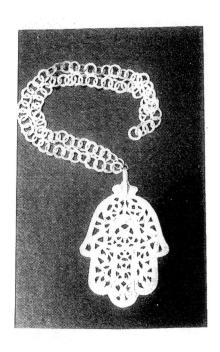

"Hand of Fatima"
Daughter of Mohamed.
Symbol of her followers

Chapter 12.

Abu Simbel
and the Nile
River and
Lake Nasser

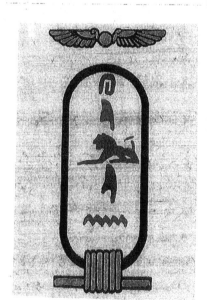

"HELEN" in hieroglyphic

Helen and Street Vendor

Chapter 12

Helen and stone carving of a Pharaoh

CHAPTER

13

Rolling Around the Med

As we were packing to leave Oxy's apartment, Buster made a suggestion.

"Before we leave North Africa, I think we should visit Tunisia. I have read that the country is a well-organized middle-class nation. And, Helen, you will like this—women have the right to vote in Tunisia."

We flew to Tunisia, rented a car, and set off on a pleasant two-week tour of the country that had once been the heart of the Roman province of Africa. We inspected well-preserved Roman ruins, villas dug deep into the ground to escape the summer heat. In Tunis, we marveled at an impressive Roman aqueduct near ancient Carthage. Familiar names on a map were now a reality.

After the arid coastline of Libya, the northern shore of Tunisia was a pleasant surprise. It was a coast clothed in a rich evergreen forest of cork oaks. We could spot beautiful homes among the trees as we drove alone.

"Some of your American movie stars have homes here," a gas station attendant told us.

Late in the day, I suggested to Buster that we find a place to eat.

"No. Not here. This looks too rich for my blood. We'll drive on."

By eight o'clock, I spoke up.

"Buster I have to eat. Let's stop at the next eating place we come to."

When we spotted one, we went in and sat down, but when we looked at the menu, we recognized nothing, all the names were strange. We pointed to an item midway down. The waiter took our order and disappeared. Half an hour later, my irritated husband spoke up.

"What's taking so long? You sure picked a dud, Helen."

Still no one came by. After another fifteen minutes, my agitated and annoyed husband walked to the kitchen door.

"Where is our meal?" he called out.

The waiter appeared. "Oh, sir, you ordered a very special vegetable that must be served cold. We had to pick it, then cook it, and now we are cooling it. It should be ready in five minutes."

We wrote down the name of what we had ordered to make sure we never ordered it again.

As we drove south, we saw oases and gardens of lush date trees. Did these dates have cholera, I wondered?

Our drive took us to the holy city of Kairouan. "Six visits to Kairouan equal one visit to Mecca," a guide told us.

To me the city looked like a dry mud-colored walled town at the edge of the sand.

On our way back to Tunis to turn in our rental car, we discovered the most beautiful little city we had ever encountered. Sidi Bou Said was a glistening white miracle, gleaming in the sunshine like a pristine jewel. Low white-washed walls were draped in dense purple, orange, and red bougainvillea vines. Masses of multicolored trailing ivy geraniums cascaded from tiny balconies. In all directions, we gazed on a panorama of glorious vibrant colors and perfumed flowers that dazzled our senses.

Everywhere we walked, the streets were swept clean, not a leaf or a scrap of debris dared to fall on Sidi Bou Said's immaculate streets. And all of this beauty was framed against the backdrop of the deep blue Mediterranean Sea.

What was next for us gypsies? Buster had a plan.

"There is an IRS (Internal Revenue Service) ruling that says if you are earning money and living outside of the United States for eighteen months, you don't have to pay income tax on those earned monies. We've been outside of the United States for eight months. We could live in

Rome for ten more months, then return to California and not owe any taxes to the IRS on the money I was paid in Libya."

So to Rome we went. The pleasant memories of Piazza Adriana drew us back to number 11. But when we met with our congenial portiere, he shook his head.

"Signora Lambrosa Kaput! Your old apartment is no longer for rent. The signora has died, and her family has sold the apartment."

"I'm sure we can find a place to rent on our own," Buster declared optimistically. "I'll check the American newspaper for rental ads. Here is one that looks promising."

"Lovely apartment in a quiet area of Rome. Available for rent for six months. US$150 a month."

25 Via Panaro, number 22 wasn't a lovely apartment, and it wasn't in a quiet area.

"But the price is right," my husband said. "I think we should take it."

We signed a six-month contract with the beaming owner who appeared to be extremely pleased with the arrangement. We moved in.

The traffic! Oh, my god, the traffic! How could we have obligated ourselves for six months to this noisy apartment? Three streets came together at the bottom of a long low hill and that's where 25 Via Panaro was, like a magnet that drew the traffic noise toward it, bounced it against the hillside, then tossed it back against our building. Nighttime was the worst. We lived in a world of cascading noise that lasted until 2:00 AM, blessedly lessened for two hours, then started up again at 4:00 AM. Buster had a hearing loss, so the constant cacophony of sound did not bother him, but I was forced to wear earplugs in order to sleep.

We had been in Rome for two months when my husband announced he was going to London.

"There is a geological conference this month and I am going. I must keep in touch with my clients and expose myself to companies where I might find future work. You can come along if you wish."

"I can't travel. I am not at all well. I feel very weary and weak. These weeks of sleepless nights are taking a toll on my tired body."

"Well, you'll have to manage here on your own because I am going."

I wakened a few mornings later to the sound of grinding machinery and sawing and loud hammering on the front of our building. Dust filled the air.

"What is going on?" I asked the building's portiere.

"Oh, this whole building is undergoing renovation, and it will be like this for six months."

The owner knew this when we rented the place. That's why he was so delighted when we signed the contract. I was disgusted by our own stupidity. When Buster returned from London, he too was furious and angry.

"We can't live like this. I'll call the owner and tell him we are moving. We can't live with this hellish noise for three more months."

When the owner met with us, he was adamant.

"No. You cannot move. You signed a legal contract valid for six months. If you leave, you owe me for three months rent."

Three more months of hell. I made a plan. "Buster did we give the owner a forwarding address?"

"No, we did not," he replied.

"Then if we were to slip out at night with our suitcases, he has no way of tracing us, does he?"

"Yeah, I guess you are right."

"Where would we go?"

"We've always talked of retiring in Mexico. We could use this as an opportunity to explore living in Mexico for seven months to finish out the eighteen-month requirement for being outside the United States."

Was there a plane that flew from Rome to Mexico City? Yes, there was a flight via the Dominican Republic leaving late in the evening. Perfect!

When the portiere left his post near the building entrance to go to supper, we locked the door to apartment 22, dropped the keys in the owner's mail slot, carried our suitcases out of the building, and hailed a taxi to take us to the international airport of Rome.

We never heard from the owner of 25 Via Panaro, apartment 22, again.

CHAPTER
14

Mexico, Our Self Imposed Exile

Buster Ivanhoe spoke fluent Spanish. His childhood had been spent in Brazil and he had worked for many years in Venezuela and Ecuador, so he felt very comfortable among the Latin peoples. I did not. The disparity between the pathetically poor and the very rich made me uncomfortable.

In Mexico City, Buster was addressed as "patrón," a term that bolstered his ego, indicating a superiority above the person speaking to him.

"I'd like to live in Mexico City," he declared. "This is where the action is."

It was also the place where the smog was, the noise, the blaring traffic, and the fecal rain that fell as a result of the overcrowded, unsanitary slums. We decided to check out Guadalajara.

We settled on Suites Marcella, a small pleasant apartment on the outskirts of Guadalajara.

On one of the first days in the apartment, my husband walked into our tiny little kitchen.

"What are you doing with all these pots?"

"I'm filling them with boiled water to make it safe for us to drink."

"Helen if we are going to live here for seven months, we should try to adapt our systems to the local water supply. The people living here drink it, so it must be safe."

But when I drank from the local water supply, minor stomach upsets plagued me.

Out of curiosity I walked up to the rooftop of our apartment where I could see a huge round tank, the apartment's water supply.

It was uncovered, open to the elements. To my absolute horror, small bugs and a dead bird were floating on the top of the water of the open tank.

For the next seven months that we lived in Suites Marcella, I continued to religiously boil all the water we used for drinking and cooking.

This was election year in Mexico, time to choose a new president. Conspicuous signs were everywhere across the city, large signs with wide bold print in gold lettering.

"Arriba y adelante con Echeverria." Translated it says "Upward and forward with Echeverria."

Echeverria won the election and, in 1970, became president of Mexico.

"Let's search out an American club so we can meet some English-speaking people," Buster said.

Boredom was a problem for foreigners in Mexico. They were not allowed to work, so many of them turned to drink. Alcohol was cheap. The first American couple we met were nondrinkers.

"We used to drink. In the late morning, if we popped in to visit a neighbor, we were offered a drink. Then we had a beer at lunch and a cocktail in the late afternoon and another before dinner. We drank with dinner and after dinner. Before long, my wife and I realized we were drunk most of the day. One day, six months ago, we swore off alcohol, and we haven't had a drink since."

Many of the Americans we met living in Guadalajara were in a self-imposed exile. For some personal reason, they had a beef with the United States. Before long, I decided they were all a bit odd. We, of course, were the normal ones!

One man cut the grass at his rented house on his knees, using small garden clippers.

"I'm bored. I had to do something to keep busy and make the job last longer."

Then there was a carpenter we met who worked full-time building an addition onto a nearby church.

"Is it true that you are buying all this lumber and materials with your own money?" I asked him.

"Helen, I can't be idle. I had to do something. Yes, I'm paying for all these supplies. Maybe God will make a special note of my good deed and put my name in the Good Book."

He smiled. "At least now when I wake up in the morning, I know I have a project ahead of me, not an empty day of nothing."

Many of the American women wore good quality clothing, but the garments were stained and spotted and should have been sent to the cleaners. But everyone was frugal, and this was a cost they could not afford.

One of the "normal" people we met was an American colonel. Colonel Hoffman and his wife had lived on Kwajalein Atoll in the Marshall Islands.

"My wife and I came to Guadalajara for a much-deserved rest. On the Atoll, I was in charge of everything and everyone. Everyone's personal problems were all brought to me to solve, and I am emotionally burned out. We have looked forward to these three quiet months where we know no one and no one knows us."

A middle-aged couple from Texas had come to Guadalajara for a three-month vacation. Anxious to make friends, we invited them to dinner at our apartment and enjoyed a pleasant evening talking about Texas politics.

Two weeks later, the lady called.

"Helen, you had us for dinner. Now we would like to reciprocate. Can you come for dinner on Sunday?"

When we arrived, our hostess said, "I do not cook so we are going out to our favorite restaurant."

At the end of an enjoyable meal, our hostess called the waiter over.

"Separate checks please," and she handed me the bill for Buster's and my meal.

She was the same lady who relayed to me with pride her experience with a local dressmaker.

"She gave me a quote for sewing me a dress and I paid her for the material, thread, and buttons. Later she said she needed six more buttons and asked me to pay her for those extra six buttons. I told her no, we made a deal and the extra buttons are your responsibility."

I looked at the diamond rings the lady was wearing.

You mean cheapskate, I thought. *This poor seamstress is struggling to support her family and you could easily afford to reimburse her for those six buttons.*

We made a point of not associating with that Texas couple again.

One of the major tequila-producing companies in Mexico was Tequila Sousa. The head of the company, Mr. Tequila Sousa, we called him, invited us to a cocktail party in honor of the American ambassador. When we arrived, we were greeted by a charming, gracious host who was outgoing and affable.

"Mr. Ambassador, may I present Mr. and Mrs. Ivanhoe?" he spoke with a winning smile as he presented us to his honored guest.

By contrast to the polished, courteous Mr. Tequila Sousa, the American ambassador seemed awkward and ill at ease, completely overshadowed by his gregarious host.

As we left the party, I commented to my husband.

"How did that dud get to be our ambassador to Mexico?"

Buster Ivanhoe was obsessed with money, saving money, making money, investing money.

"If we think we may live in Mexico when I retire, we should invest some money here as a long-term commitment."

My husband found a real-estate agent he liked, a seemingly knowledgeable young man who spoke excellent English and with whom he felt comfortable.

"Americans cannot own land on the beachfront, but there is some property inland that shows great promise for future growth. We could be partners, and you could invest your money there."

The young man sounded believable, so we invested $1,000 in partnership with Snr. Rodregas, our hopes high for future benefits.

It turned out that the land we thought we had purchased was ejido land, land that in Mexican law is a land set aside for use by the native people of a town or a pueblo.

We never saw our $1,000 again and Snr. Rodregas, our believable real-estate partner, faded from sight.

Our self-imposed seven-month exile had drawn to a close.

"We will remain out of the United States an extra five days over the required eighteen-month absence just to ensure I have met the IRS exception from paying income tax on the monies I earned in Libya," my husband declared.

When emancipation day finally arrived, we decided to return to Bakersfield.

"That's where the center of California oil activity is, and maybe by now people have forgotten that my son was sent to juvenile hall."

On February 5, 1970, when I stepped onto the tarmac at Los Angeles airport, I wanted to kiss the ground in grateful relief.

Rentals were scarce in Bakersfield, so we had to take whatever we could find. After three moves, we found a pleasant apartment not far from the Oxy office. The apartments were built like row houses, all alike, all joined together by common walls.

But those walls were not well insulated, and we could hear the private goings-on of the handsome young bachelor next to us, his visiting lady friends, the noisy toilet flushes in the middle of the night, personal sounds I did not want to hear, but from which there was no escape.

If we could hear him, then he must be able to hear us, so it was an even trade.

One of his young lady friends apparently decided she was moving in with the handsome young bachelor. One afternoon, I watched her carrying suitcases and belongings into his apartment. When he returned from work early one evening, I heard a loud outburst.

"What are you doing here?"

"We get along so well, I thought we should live together."

"Well, you thought wrong. You can't live here. It is late, so you can spend the night here, but be out of here, bag and baggage when I come back from the office tomorrow."

The following evening when the young man stepped inside his apartment, loud audible voices came through the walls from the upstairs bedroom.

"I told you to get out."

"Why don't you want me here? Tell me. I have to know. Why can't I live with you?"

"Get out! Get out! I don't want you here. Get out."

Crash! Bang! Crash! The young man had opened an upstairs window and was throwing all the young woman's possessions to the concrete pad below.

If he thought that was the end of the young lady, he was wrong. The next morning, he got into his car, started backing out of the carport, then realized his exit was blocked. The young banished woman had parked her car immediately behind his so that it was impossible for him to move his automobile out of the carport.

"Please move your car. I have to get to work. Please move."

Nothing. No reaction from the woman.

"Move, please. I have a job. I have to get to work. Please, please move."

No reaction from the rejected woman.

"Damn it! I have to get to work. Please move your car."

"Move!"

The young man got out of his car, strode angrily over to the woman's car, and after several minutes of gestures and loud voices, she eventually drove off in a cloud of dust.

I never saw or heard her return to our next-door neighbor's apartment.

My husband and I were at an impasse. I wanted to buy a house; he did not.

"It is more advantageous to rent and invest your money at a high interest rate than it is to put that money into a home." He repeatedly and positively voiced that opinion.

Finally, after several years, he relented, and we signed the papers to buy a small condo, he with great reluctance and I with great relief. At last we had a pied-à-terre, a foot on earth at 6000 Cypress Point Drive. At last, we owned a home.

CHAPTER
15

Bogotá, Colombia

"Helen, why don't you take a real-estate course and become a real-estate salesperson? You would have a built-in clientele. Oxy people are always being transferred, and new people are constantly moving in. Think of the money you could make for us."

Determined to be a success, I launched into an energizing career in real estate. The more hours I put in, the more successful I became. It was satisfying but tiring.

When Buster announced that Oxy had again offered him a seven-month job, this time in Colombia, South America, I was pleased at the prospect of a vacation.

"It's much the same deal as before," Buster told me. "Oxy wants me to fill in as acting chief geophysicist while they clear up all the paperwork for their permanent man."

Since we were living in a condo in a homeowners association, there was nothing to do but pay seven months condo dues in advance, lock the front door, and leave.

"We've made your reservations at the best hotel in Bogotá," Oxy's travel department told us. "The Tecandama is where all the gringos stay, but watch out for pickpockets. That hotel is notorious as the spot where these clever guys hang out waiting for foreigners. They seem to especially go for men's watches, so be extra careful."

We registered at the impressive Tecandama Hotel. As representatives of Occidental Petroleum, we were given preferential treatment. When we entered our spacious room, I gasped in pleased surprise at the huge bouquet of red roses on the coffee table. I counted twenty-four blooms.

"Bienvenida a Bogotá, Señora Helen," the card read. It was signed "Armando."

"Who is Armando?" I asked Buster.

"Oh, he's a geologist you met at a convention, but don't get any ideas."

Buster left the room to run a quick errand. He returned, obviously agitated and annoyed.

"Well, that didn't take long."

"What happened?"

"A guy in front of the hotel reached out to grab my wristwatch, but it caught in the sleeve of my wool sweater, and as he pulled on my watch, my sleeve pulled and stretched. I yelled, but he kept jerking and pulling and stretching my sleeve until he finally gave up, let go, and disappeared."

"Did he get your watch?"

"No, it is still here, tangled up in my stretched wool sleeve."

The next day, anxious to explore Bogotá, I set out for the Plaza Principal, the main plaza of the city. All afternoon I wandered among the fascinating stores, the ornate cathedral, and the intriguing antique shops, oblivious to time until I realized the church clock had just struck six and dusk was gathering. As I turned and walked hurriedly in the direction of our hotel, out of nowhere, I was suddenly surrounded by a crowd of shouting students waving placards.

"Down with America," they screamed.

I was caught inexplicably in the yelling mob, swept along by the inertia of the moving mass. The fervor of these marching students frightened me.

"Down with America. Down with America," they chanted all around me. For the first time in all my world travels, I was afraid. Slowly, I worked my way to the edge of the screaming mob, hoping no one would decide I was an American and make me the focus of their anger. Finally, on a quiet street, I stood there shaking, unfamiliar with the city and not sure how to make my way back to the hotel.

Reason told me to follow streets parallel to the main avenue I had walked earlier, but when a street ended in a brick wall, I panicked. Which way? Which way? The shouts of the students saved me. I guessed they were marching toward the Tecandama Hotel so I followed alongside streets in the direction of the yelling. When at last, I could see the Tecandama ahead of me, there were the students waving their placards and chanting, "Down with America. Down with America."

No one paid any attention to me as I pushed my way through the crowd and gratefully entered the hotel lobby.

A few days later, I asked the hotel concierge, "Have you any suggestion of an interesting place to visit that I could walk to?"

"Oh, yes, Señora. There is a new modern shopping center only a mile northwest of here that you might enjoy."

Bakersfield didn't have any shopping centers as attractive as this Bogotá complex. Huge leafy trees grew up to the second story from below. Shops sold stylish attractive clothing. Pretty, shapely young ladies walked about in elegant high heels. Looking at these charming girls, I could understand why so many American geologists came back to California with pretty Colombian wives.

Buster was waiting for me in our hotel room when I returned.

"Pack up your stuff. I have rented an apartment."

"You what?"

"I rented us a place, and we can move in today, so hurry and get your things."

I was stunned, hurt, insulted, indignant, and very angry. He had rented a place to live without me seeing it. Surely he could have waited until I returned from my excursion.

"Why didn't you wait until I could see this place?"

"Look! I make the decisions in this family and that's that."

There was nothing I could do but accept his decision, but my anger roiled inside me.

Maybe this will be a nice place, I told myself. It wasn't!

The apartment was unattractive and bleak and not in a pleasant area. There was nothing, absolutely nothing going for it, except that the rent was cheap. The wall-to-wall carpeting was thin tufts of discolored and grease-stained matting. The kitchen was dark, stained, and sticky. But it was the bed I cursed the months we lived there. There were no box springs and only a thin tufted mattress on top of coiled ropelike springs, fastened at the headboard and footboard in parallel lines, six inches apart across the width of the double bed. When we lay down, we both rolled into the hollow in the middle. My husband, being the heaviest had a major advantage over my slight frame, instantly falling asleep and snoring as I lay fuming. Next morning when I pulled the mattress off, I could see that someone had broken apart cardboard boxes and spread them across the springs in an attempt to firm up the bed. It hadn't worked.

Some rental! After a month of pleading with our landlady, she agreed to have the carpets shampooed. What was left after the carpets were cleaned was almost nothing but the backing, so thin had been the carpeting.

During the time we spent in Bogotá, we never had guests come to this rental, so ashamed was I of my husband's choice.

A letter to our daughter in California.

Bogotá, Colombia
January 1, 1980

Dear Cheryl,

When you live here, there is never a dull moment. And you think you can plan ahead but you really can't.

Take for instance yesterday. There was a knock at the door of our apartment and a man stood there with a piece of paper in his hand. "This bill is for two months of lights," he said. "But we have been here only ten days" I said. Then he spoke rapidly in Spanish, but I did not understand. "It is not my bill, so I won't pay it," I said. Not too much later, I went to turn the light on in the bathroom. Guess what? That's right—no lights! Quite a direct cause-and-effect situation. I called Buster at the office. His secretary called our landlady, and eventually, we got the lights back on. But now we have no hot water. The maid looked at the water heater and shook her head. She called the portiere, and he looked at the water heater, got out a screwdriver, and he shook his head. Now, I gather they are going to call the "secretariat" and get the "administration" to come and look at it.

We have been here in the apartment nearly two weeks. When we moved in, the landlady promised to have our rugs shampooed (they are filthy, greasy, and food-spotted and very unpleasant looking). And she promised to have the couch and chairs repaired. The springs are all broken. Guess what? The rugs aren't cleaned yet, and the chairs aren't repaired yet, but today at 2:00 PM a man is scheduled to arrive and clean the rugs. I wonder if he will really, really come.

We have found only one shop that sells milk. It comes in a white plastic sack. You cut off the end, pour the milk into a pitcher, and throw away the sack. But if you get to the store too late in the day, the milk is all sold out. Yesterday I got there too late to buy milk, so this morning before breakfast, your dad went to buy milk and he was first in line. Guess what? He got there *too early*, and the milk had not yet arrived.

Fortunately, we eat out most of the time. People here are pleasant to us, and we do a lot of sightseeing on weekends.

Your father and I send our love. Keep well!

Mother

The Colombian geologists were friendly and outgoing, often inviting us to dinners in their lovely, spacious homes. One evening as we were being entertained in the formal living room, robbers stealthily entered through a back side door, moved silently into the upstairs bedrooms, and robbed the family's jewelry without any of us having heard a sound.

Buster's secretary Angela, a very congenial young woman, offered us suggestions of places to see.

"Helen, you and Mr. Ivanhoe must visit our Gold Museum. Bogotá is very proud of this exceptional display of our country's national treasures."

At the Gold Museum, we were led into a small lobby, doors closed behind us, two huge doors in front of us stood closed. So where was this famous gold display? Lights were turned off, and we stood in total darkness. Then we heard the big doors in front of us sliding open. Lights went on. We gasped in surprised amazement. We stood speechless in front of a large room glistening, shining, sparkling with gleaming gold objects in front of us, along every wall, everywhere we turned to look. Could this be real? Was this a cinema trick? Could there be so many gold objects all in one place?

Gold statues of Colombian gods, gold masks, gold boxes and trays, a variety of gold bowls and vases, a huge collection of gold jewelry, necklaces, earrings, bracelets, pectorals, wide gold collars, animal figures, serpents and weird species we could not identify.

Over 14,000 gold pieces were on display—an overwhelming sight.

A recorded voice brought us back to reality.

"Please enter our museum and carefully walk about, but do not touch these previous objects." It was real gold. All those objects were real gold.

Stories of El Dorado, the Gold Man, had lured the Spanish Conquistadors to Colombia. The indigenous local rulers had covered their bodies in gold dust then bathed in sacred lakes. Enflamed by a desire to locate El Dorado, the Spanish searched relentlessly for the gold of Colombia, from the High Andes to the Amazon basin, from the shores of the Atlantic to the Pacific.

In Cartagena in 1533, the conquistadors built a treasure port to collect Colombian gold to send to Spain along a sea route that came to be known as the Spanish Main. Cartagena became the most important city in the New World. Its walls were forty feet thick, twenty-nine forts protected it from pirates, chains were strung across port entrances to deter enemy ships from entering. It seemed impregnable.

When Angela suggested she could arrange airfare to Cartagena on a weekend, we eagerly accepted. As Buster and I walked atop the city's thick wide walls, I felt a gentle breeze constantly blowing evenly and steadily, on and on.

"These are the westerlies," Buster explained. These are the winds the Spanish ships depended on to bring their precious cargo to Spain."

Turbulent and violent periods existed between the local Indian population and the Spanish explorers until 1819 when Simón Bolívar, at the Battle of Boyáca, expelled the Spanish authorities. I had read of the Puente de Boyáca (the bridge of Boyáca) where the final battle took place. Expecting to see a huge impressive bridge, I was surprised to see that the puente was a small, narrow bridge over a narrow stream. Things don't have to be big to be important.

Angela, ever helpful, gave us suggestions of interesting villages to visit for weekends of sightseeing. In 1980, Colombia was still a relatively safe country, and we never felt in harm's way. We were always treated politely as we walked about, admiring village squares, impressive churches, masses of colorful bougainvillea, bamboo groves, and colorful flowering trees.

"Stay away from Cali," Angela warned us. "It is the drug capital of Colombia." We followed her advice and avoided Cali.

During the weekdays while my husband was at work, I wandered among Bogotá's fascinating shops, so much variety—a huge antique store, next to a shop crammed with weird herbal remedies, next to a colorful fabric store. Always something new.

Cotton yardage trimmed with wide borders of gold and silver threads appealed to me so I bought three lengths, enough to make three floor-length skirts.

"Angela, do you know of a seamstress who could sew this lovely yardage into skirts for me?"

"Oh, yes, Helen. I know an excellent seamstress."

When I went to visit Señora Maria, she admired my fabric and listened intently as I told her of the simple styles I wanted.

"Come back next Friday and your three long skirts will be ready." She smiled.

On Friday when I arrived for my skirts, Señora Maria glowed.

"Oh, look what I have created for you."

She held the skirts up, one by one. Each was an extreme creation of pleats, flounces, bustles, and irregular hemlines, not at all what I had envisioned.

"Do you like them?" the proud seamstress asked.

I stared at my once pretty fabrics now sewn into such weird creations. I was surprised and disappointed. What to say? I had to say something.

"This is so different from what I had envisioned," I mumbled.

"Oh, Senora, you are too young and pretty to wear plain styles. I am an artist, and I created for you individualistic, unique, one of a kind designs for you to wear with pride. Artists create, and I used my artistic talents to create for you."

When we returned to California those three extreme, artistic creations of Señora Maria were all donated to Goodwill Industries.

"Oxy's new man has arrived and will be taking over on Monday. Before we leave, I'd like to visit and thank the Colombian geologists who have been so very gracious to us. And you can even thank Armando for those roses he sent you when we arrived."

One of the geologists we visited commented, "Have you seen the striking new place your Oxy geologist has rented? It is a modern marvel. In the living room, the walls of glass go from ceiling to floor. When I stood there, I felt I was about to fall to the street below, so clean and clear was the glass."

Buster's aim in renting our tacky place had been to show Oxy how frugal he was—how much money he could save the company.

This Occidental Oil Company's manager's aim was to demonstrate to the Colombian authorities how successful and prosperous Oxy was. His magnificent home gave the impression of a company with the financial resources to meet the challenges of petroleum exploration in Colombia.

"We are successful. Look at what we can afford," his residence shouted.

"Angela will prepare our tickets back to Bakersfield as soon as we tell her which airline we prefer to fly. She gave me the various flight schedules to look over."

Flying Bogotá to Los Angeles first class was a rare treat for me. I looked forward to the attentive service and delicious food that airlines served their prime passengers in 1980.

"Why don't we select an airline with three meals during the flight so we can enjoy breakfast, lunch, and dinner on our return to Los Angeles?" I asked Buster.

We carefully studied the brochures and picked Braniff. As soon as we stepped aboard the plane, polite and gracious stewardesses made us feel important as they attended to our every request.

"Look how pretty these young ladies are," Buster said. "So easy on the eyes."

We ate everything on the breakfast menu with great gusto, drank a bottle of wine, and fell asleep. When we awoke it was midafternoon. Oh! Oh! We had missed lunch. We went back to sleep. When dinnertime came, we still were not hungry and skipped that meal as well.

Our clever plan to eat three big meals had not panned out, but we had a restful and relaxed flight.

I was reminded of the story a geologist friend told me.

"I was sent by my company to Mideastern and Eastern world capitals to meet with government officials and negotiate for oil concessions. I decided to take my sixteen-year-old son with me as an opportunity to expose him to different worlds. Everywhere we went we traveled first class, stayed in the best hotels, and were entertained by dignitaries. When we were flying back home, I asked him about his experiences.

"Well, son, what have you learned on this trip?"

"When I graduate, I think I'll become a geologist. I like the lifestyle," he replied.

Los Angeles to Bakersfield in a noisy little plane—we were finally back to familiar ground at Kern county airport.

As we walked to the taxi stand, I saw that the next taxi in line was a big older car, somewhat beat up, a relic from better days.

I hesitated.

"We must take it," Buster said. "It's the courteous thing to do."

Our young driver matched his car, a baseball cap and a rumpled T-shirt with slogans.

As we drove along, my husband and I noticed changes that had taken place since we had left Bakersfield.

"Look, that three-story apartment house is finally completed."

"And see that big house going up on that lot that was vacant when we last drove by?"

"You guys been gone a long time?" our driver asked.

"Seven months," I replied.

"Where have you guys been?"

"We've been in Bogotá."

"Oh."

"That's in Colombia," I added.

"Oh."

"That's in South America. We are returning from South America."

"Jeez! South America. Gosh! You guys sure have been a long way from home."

The taxi stopped in front of 6000 Cypress Point Drive. The lawn was neatly mowed, the sidewalks were swept, the hedges trimmed and pink begonias were blooming near the front door. We were back at our pied-à-terre, our foot on earth.

No more moving for the Ivanhoes. This is where we wanted to live. Stability at long, long last, or so I hoped.

Something was bothering my husband. He often sat, staring ahead at nothing in particular, quiet and withdrawn. One afternoon, he sprang up from his chair.

"Ever since Rod was sent to juvenile hall, I have never felt comfortable in Bakersfield. Too many bad memories come back to me. I see no future prospects for me in the petroleum industry here in this county. I would like to retire to Santa Barbara on the coast where the weather is more agreeable and leave all those bad memories behind me."

We sold 6000 Cypress Point Drive the day I listed it on the market. Our neighbor across the street bought it for his wife without even coming over to inspect it.

"I'm dying of cancer, and I want my wife to have a nice rental to add to her income when I'm gone," he told me.

Some old routine. Sort. Pack. Call the movers. Fill out change of address forms for our next place, 715 Avenida Pequena, Santa Barbara. Someday, I'm going to count the number of places all around the world where I have lived.

149

Bogotá
 Colombia
Chapter 15
Museo de Oro
Colombian
Gods in solid gold.

Lush vegetation

Bogotá Famous statue in park

Chapter 16

A busy real estate
saleslady in Bakersfield,
California

Helen and Hugh
Smart in Santa
Barbara.

Finis, Death, Divorce, Suicide

Retirement did not agree with Bus Ivanhoe. No job. No work. No close friends. Empty hours ahead of him each day and time on his hands.

I became his enemy, the focus of his discontent and anger. When his son, Rod died at forty-three years of age, from a self-inflicted gunshot wound, Bus withdrew into his own dark cloud, emerging only to scream at me and flay his fists.

"I feel like hitting you."

Physical and mental abuse was not new to me, but over the years, I had always excused his outbursts.

"He is upset. He is worried because he has no work or income. Things will get better if I try to please him more." Or maybe he has a medical problem that could be treated. Maybe there is a drug that could help him. I resolved to bravely approach my husband with a suggestion.

"Buster, please consider going to a doctor. Perhaps there is some physical reason while you feel so distraught."

My suggestion was met with a sneer. "There is nothing wrong with me. I don't go to doctors. You are the one who should go. You are the one with problems. You are unreasonable, antagonistic, and impossible to live with, not I."

As the weeks went by, things got worse. I lived in uneasy fear of his sudden, violent, unpredictable anger. One afternoon, for no provocation I could determine, he stood across from me at the kitchen counter, screaming into my face.

"You are stupid! You can't manage on your own. If it wasn't for me, you wouldn't be anything. You have no friends. You couldn't live a day without my help. You are nothing. You never did anything worthwhile in your life. You're pathetic."

I looked at the face of my husband, contorted with hatred, directed at me.

Inside of me, a quiet, firm voice said, "You don't have to live like this."

Memories I had kept submerged for years suddenly flooded over me—the times he had angrily pummeled his clenched fists against the sides of my head (always where the bruises would not show), the times he pulled my long hair violently jerking my head from side to side.

My life was in peril. It was time to go!

Carefully and cautiously, I needed to lay out plans for a divorce. Where to start? Where to turn? Ashamed to tell any of my friends, I turned to the Woman's Shelter of Santa Barbara.

"This is a classic case of spousal abuse. You need to get out of there before you are lying on the floor, bruised and battered with broken bones. Protect yourself and your future. Once you leave, you may never see the inside of that house again. Rent yourself a small storage unit and secretly put in your most treasured items and copies of all your financial papers."

And that is what I did.

Because our finances were routinely and carefully scrutinized by my husband, I knew I should copy every financial paper and be aware of all aspects of our estate. When the time came for the final divorce settlement, he could not take advantage of my "pathetic" naivete. Whenever I removed a paper from a file to copy it, I was nervous and uneasy until I slipped it back into its proper slot. Surreptitiously in those brief periods when Buster was away from the house, items were taken to my storage unit—my valued featherweight portable Singer sewing machine, a few basic clothes, precious photo albums of my life's history—all things that would not be obviously missed from the house.

At a bank, some distance from our house, I opened a checking account and rented a safe-deposit box with specific instructions to the young lady bank manager that under no circumstances was any correspondence to be sent to Avenida Pequena, my home address.

"I will personally come to the bank every Friday to check for any notices."

"There is something going on here," the bank manager said. "What is it you are doing?"

"I'm filing for divorce without my husband's knowledge. I'm afraid of my husband. The Woman's Shelter is counseling me, and they have warned me that sometimes when a man learns his wife is leaving, he can become so irrational that he rips up his wife's clothes, smashes the furniture, and physically attacks her."

The bank manager called over another young woman.

"This is my assistant manager."

The two young ladies spoke quietly together, then both of them turned and shook my hand.

"Your secret is safe with us."

In the Santa Barbara News Press, I found an ad for a woman attorney specializing in divorce. Time after time I traipsed the stairs to her upstairs office.

"Where are you going to live while this divorce is being finalized?" she asked.

Blessed are those of us who have a supportive family.

"Of course you can stay with me while you are getting your divorce," my sister Valeria immediately replied. "You can stay with me here in Vernon, British Columbia as long as you like."

The reply from my youngest brother, John in Ontario, Canada was the same.

"Marianne and I welcome you to stay with us anytime."

Ed, my bachelor brother was equally supportive.

"Sister, you can live here as long as you like but just don't try cleaning up my shack. Nobody touches my shack but me."

It was time to take friends into my confidence and blessed are those of us who have loyal friends to turn to. I turned to Marsha, a long-time friend.

"I am going to Vernon, British Columbia, to live with my sister for six months, and my husband is not to know where I am. Can I use your address for a change of address?"

"Of course! Direct correspondence to my post office box. Give me your sister's address, and I'll forward your mail every week. Just leave me enough money for postage."

Next I spoke to Dorrie, a respected older friend, knowing she had a huge back garden hidden from the street.

"May I store my little red Toyota Corolla in your garden until the divorce is finalized?"

"Of course, but I suggest you check with the Toyota garage to see if you should take any special precautions before you leave that pretty little car for six months."

Instructions from the Toyota mechanic were simple. "When you are ready to leave your car in your friend's garden, top off the gas tank with the highest octane gas. Park it, disengage the negative from the battery, lock the car, cover it with a car cover, and you'll have no problem when you return in six months."

Not wanting there to be any credit card records, I purchased a one-way airplane ticket to Vernon, British Columbia, Canada, with cash. In 1993 when the world was safer, that did not raise any alarms, as it would today after 9/11.

The scoldings, the shouting, the diatribe and tirades, the constant castigation from my husband continued, but now I had wrapped myself in an invisible cloak of impenetrability.

"You aren't listening to me," he often screamed.

No, Buster, I wasn't listening to you anymore.

My attorney told me I could legally withdraw a sum of money from our joint savings account in Maryland.

"We'll inform the judge what you have done, and it will be stated in the divorce papers."

When I tore off the top check from our joint account, I was trembling. What if he saw the missing check? Had I been smarter, I would have removed the check from the bottom of the pack, but that did not occur to me at the time.

At the bank I spoke with both managers. "Please do all you can to clear this check and deposit it to my account ASAP before my husband finds it missing and puts a stop order on it. I'll be at the Woman's Shelter in two days. There is only one telephone there. When this check has been cleared and is in my account, will you phone and let me know? Just say, 'All clear' and do not elaborate."

The ladies agreed. That is what they did. To this day, I recall my intense relief when I heard those words, "All clear." Now I had some money Buster could not hide from me.

During the years I had lived in Goleta, my neighbor, Alene, had become a caring friend.

"Alene, I need your help. I'm leaving Buster but I don't want him to know when or where I'm going. Can I leave a small suitcase and my overnight bag with you? And will you meet me at Tucker's Grove Park on Friday at 10:00 AM and turn them over to me?"

Friday morning, I announced to my husband, "I'm going to spend the day volunteering at the Natural History Museum. Don't wait dinner for me."

On September 27, 1993, I picked up my purse, and without a backward glance at a house full of memories, I walked rapidly and resolutely to my car. Over and over, I had mentally rehearsed the steps I would follow. There was no turning back. I met Alene at Tucker's Grove Park, picked up my bags, hugged her, then drove to the Santa Barbara Courthouse where I signed the divorce papers. I walked away with an overwhelming sense of relief and a touch of sadness for a forty-five-year marriage that was no more, a marriage that had failed. It was done! It was all over!

From there, I drove to Dorrie's and parked my Toyota in a secluded corner of her big yard next to a tall oak tree. I phoned the Women's Shelter.

"I am ready to be picked up."

"Have your friend drive you to the McDonald's on State Street, and we'll pick you up there."

That night, safe in a tiny upstairs room, I slept soundly and peacefully, knowing I was no longer subject to Buster's sudden and violent angry moods.

The debt I owe my sister Valeria during the six months I lived with her cannot be put into words. With infinite patience, she listened politely to the repeated accounts of my trials with Buster, her kindness and sympathetic support never faltering. The blessed peace of tranquil days in her calm house devoid of fear and unease—each day was a healing gift. Life was good!

Her concern for my health and well-being was evidenced the morning I liberally sprayed myself with an expensive perfume my friend Dorrie had given me. Expecting a compliment but receiving none, I sprinkled more perfume on my body. Still no reaction from Valeria, so I applied a third generous dose of my costly perfume. That did bring a response.

"Helen, are you feeling well?"

"Yes, why do you ask?"

"Well, I have read that when people have certain diseases, a strong odor accompanies that disease. I detected an unusual odor surrounding you when you came into the room. I am concerned. Are you well?"

"Yes, I am well, but a long shower bath is in order." We laughed when I told her about my liberal use of my expensive perfume.

There was one more debt to repay when I returned to Santa Barbara. As a show of gratitude, I invited all the ladies who had been so supportive during my divorce proceedings to a dinner at Goleta's finest restaurant.

"Order anything and everything that appeals to you," I announced. "This is my simple way of thanking all of you for your helpful friendship when I was in desperate need of your support."

The two lady bank managers laughed.

"It is not often we get taken to dinner by our customers. We are pleased that everything has worked out so well for you."

"Yes, Helen, I am relieved that you finally divorced Buster," one of my guests added.

"But—what took you so long?"

With support from my loyal friends and my sympathetic family, I made a new life for myself. In 1995, I met a man who looked at me with kind eyes. In 1998, Hugh Taylor Smart and I were married in front of beaming friends and family who laughingly blew soap bubbles in our direction as we walked happily down the aisle of the Unity Church of Santa Barbara.

In 2003, L. F. (Bus) Ivanhoe, geologist, geophysicist, oceanographer, and historian, committed suicide, a tragic end to a once productive life.

He was widely known in the petroleum industry as a well-published author of articles emphasizing the world's declining oil reserves. His memory lives on in his daughter Cheryl of Ojai, California.

One more final move. A final resting place for this rolling stone gypsy.

In Santa Barbara there is a beautiful cemetery high on a hill. To the south is a view of the Pacific Ocean and the offshore islands. To the north is a view of the three-thousand-foot-high Santa Ynez Mountains.

In the cemetery is a quiet corner, the Sunrise Urn Garden. In the garden is an oak tree. Near the tree is a bench. A few feet beyond is a granite memorial.

Helen Veronica Liss Smart
Feb. 4, 1927–
Bound forever by a love found
in the autumn of our lives.
Hugh Taylor Smart
Jan. 19, 1930–

About the Author

Helen Liss Ivanhoe Smart was born on an isolated homestead in Northern Alberta, Canada. At 19 years of age she began her teaching career with eight grades in a log cabin schoolhouse. In 1949 she married L. F. Ivanhoe, a petroleum geologist, and moved to Taft, California. She has lived in Libya, Israel, Turkey, Italy, Colombia, and Mexico.

Her work has been published in Saturday Evening Post, Sunset Magazine, and various children's magazines. In 2007 she wrote "The Intrepid Fox", the story of her family's challenging pioneer life in Northern Alberta. In 2011, a second book, "Lord Save Me From Taft" a tale of a young bride's struggle to adapt to life in a foreign land was published by Shoreline Press.

Today she lives in Santa Barbara, California with her husband Hugh Smart, where she is active in community affairs when she is not busy in her garden.